How to Give the Million View TEDx Talk

Lance Allred

How to Give the Million View TEDx Talk

What is Your Polygamy?

L SQUARED
L Squared Productions
Copyright
2017

L Squared Productions 2017

ISBN 978-1546403760

Table of Contents

Part 1

Lance Allred

Part 2
Partners and Mentors

"Awakening the Roaring Lion"
Dennis Allen, MBA

"Planes and Train…wrecks"
Christoph Merrill

"Discovering Clarity"
Christy Foster

"Anatomy of a TEDx Talk"
David K Brake

"A Space Shuttle Tile, A Philosopher, A New Life Form & My Good
Friend, Lance Allred"
Dave Murray

"Heal Thyself"
Dr. Jaynee Poulson, PhD

Part 3-
Coaching and Editing

Editing a TEDx submission with Michael Page

"Shots"
A TEDx Draft By - Bosten Van Der Veur- College Student

"Critiquing an Existing TEDx Talk: *We Will Go On Loving Ourselves*"
Kambridge Van Der Veur

Part 4-
What is YOUR Polygamy?

"Mining the Walls"
Matthew Langston

"My Miracle"
Kelli Davis

"Wings"
NiKohl M. Cotton

Dedicated to Simon.
Sweet Boy,
I have no words.

Part One

Lance Allred

Prologue

Sweaty palms. Sweaty feet. Heart beating like a Goth kick drum.

Yep... we're really doin' it. We... are... really... doin'... it.

Pacing backstage like a taller Honey Boo-Boo, I am doing my best to recall my pregame ritual from my basketball days, something I did for 10 years as a professional basketball player around the world. And yet, none of those tricks seem to be working.

Wait... the 10x10x10 breathing! Haven't tried that yet!

I find a dark corner to lie down and stretch my arms above my head. I inhale a slow, deep breath, counting to ten... but my constricted and panicked lungs fill up fully at the "6" count.

I hold the breath and begin counting to "10" but my lungs don't have that much air. I release it, with the naive hope that I will slowly exhale to the count of "10."

Fail: my lungs empty completely by the third count.

I try the cycle again. A little better the second go round. All the while, the backstage crew pass by, most too scrambled to notice the fallen 7-foot timber frame (that is me) hidden in the corner... I am wearing black, this is true.

But someone does notice me and taps my foot with theirs.

Doing my best to not appear as an annoyed diva, I sit up and flick my hearing aids on and wait for them to fire up.

There is always an awkward 3-second count before the hearing aids fully charge on, and by then people are already in their second or third sentence, so I do in fact, have to do my best "diva" and hold up my index finger as to tell the lady inquiring of me to hold that thought.

Hearing aids give their little jingle and they are on!

Lady smiles at me, "Are you ok? I wasn't sure to bother you, as I thought you might be meditating, but wanted to make sure you didn't pass out. Going first is never easy."

I give my own polite smile, "I am good. Thank you. Maybe we should put a tube sock on my shoe." I mean it kindly and she laughs and moves on.

Yep... I'm going first. No pressure.

Chapter 1
So, You Want to Give a TEDx Talk?

I get it. You are a TEDster. You have watched most, if not all the "good" TEDx Talks: Amy Cuddy, Melissa Gilbert, Sir Ken Robinson, all of those other Million View TEDx Talks that inspire you.

So now you feel like, *Hey, I can do the same thing. I want to inspire the people. And I have a great idea worth sharing.*

The thing about TEDx Talks though is that you have to realize everyone has a story, yet a great story is not enough for a TEDx Talk. You have to have an idea worth spreading, something different.

*Note: The trademark of TED: *"Ideas worth spreading."* Not, Stories worth sharing. Always remember this.

If you already have a great idea, then you are ahead of the game.

But if all you have is a story, you have to ask yourself how you are going to flip it around to make it unique, so that it applies to everyone else?

You have to convert and translate your story into an idea.

What is the difference?

A story is merely a recalling or narration of an experience.

An idea is something that triggers listeners to think about and analyze a topic in a very new and different way. Or at least an original idea.

Once you have your original idea, you are on the right track.

Granted, your idea can't hit 100% of the listeners. Furthermore, it's not going to inspire people 100% either, but if you achieve about 50% influence and impact on the people who listen to you talk, that's an idea worth sharing.

1

When I retired from basketball in April of 2015, I decided, *"So yeah, let's become a motivational speaker."*

As though somehow it would be easy.

It wasn't really in my plan to retire at the age of 34. But I was going through a divorce and I didn't want to be away from my son. There weren't a lot of options. But I figured I had a set of skills that would apply to the world of public speaking.

Having been on a book tour in 2009 with HarperCollins for my book LONGSHOT, I realized I actually enjoyed public speaking.

Who knew? The deaf kid becomes the media guy for his basketball teams?

It's kind of a funny thing that happened.

I have had many people come up to me and ask,

"Well, with your hearing loss, and you being an introvert, isn't it kind of strange that you'd be a motivational speaker?'

It's fair to ask, but when I'm on stage, I don't have to worry about anyone talking; all I have to do is talk.

I don't have to worry about listening or hearing anybody. Being on a stage is very comfortable for me, far more comfortable than being in some fancy wine tasting soiree, with everyone's pinkies raised high.

Speaking comes naturally to me even though I was in speech therapy for fifteen years, enabling me to speak this way. It's something I've always wanted to do. It is in my nature to be an orator, with some of it passed down through my genetics and DNA

Some already know that my grandfather was Rulon Allred. He was "the prophet" and founder of a polygamous commune in rural Montana. He named his group the Apostolic United Brethren. I never knew him. He was killed, murdered, four years before I was born.

But, I was raised in his dream of Pinesdale, Montana. From everything that I know and understand about my grandfather, he was a very charismatic man-

You had to be in order to get seven thousand people to give you all their money and seven women to marry you.

No doubt, he had charisma. He was charming and he knew how to talk. And he knew how to influence people via public speaking. I've never seen him in a video or audio recording of him speaking, but I do know that he was quite powerful in his oration, according to people's recollections of him.

I did, however, get to watch my father speak.

My father is a brilliant orator and he inherited the same charm that my grandfather had. However, my father never really had any desire to be the head of the Allred religious group even though many wanted him to be so.

My father, Vance, was a schoolteacher, as well the scholar and doctrinaire of our polygamous commune. Growing up, I watched him on the stage in church or other religious gatherings. I watched how his body posture and stance would just transform.

His confidence boomed.

Off the stage, my father is a very quiet, reserved and introverted man, but once he gets on stage, he flips a switch and then the oration and power come through.

I also watched him when he was a schoolteacher for twenty plus years, teaching history in Missoula, Montana, and then in Salt Lake City, Utah. My father is a master speaker and he knows how to capture the imagination of others.

So, yes, you can say it is somewhat in my nature to be an orator, to stand on the stage, talk and communicate with people. Furthermore, as far as deaf polygamist kids making the NBA, I have sort of cornered the market.

I have that going for me.

I don't think there will ever be another me on this planet that has that kind of background and so my story is unique. It is very different. You really can't make it up.

But I also knew that my story alone wasn't enough for a TEDx talk. How was I going to flip it? How was I going to make it unique?

This was the challenge.
And this is your challenge.

What is your idea?
Do you even have an idea?
Do you even care or are you willing to create any idea just to get on a TEDx Stage?
Is your idea new? Something no one else has thought of?
What is it teaching?
Is it enough to keep an audience fascinated?
These are questions you should be asking yourself.

Chapter 2
Head, Heart, and Soul

The world of motivational and public speaking is a very interesting one. It is competitive - extremely competitive and not as altruistic as we might have once hoped.

A lot of people stand on the stage and they motivate and inspire and create an idea of who they are, or maybe just who you want them to be, but once you see them off the stage, they're completely different people. I saw this a lot with my basketball coaches, but as far as "altruistic speakers?" I guess I didn't want to believe it.

It was a challenging adjustment for me when I retired from basketball. I was getting advice from professional speakers whom I thought were mentors. I realized they actually weren't. They were claiming to be something that they were not.

With my wacky crazy story of being the first deaf (polygamist) kid to make the NBA, I was threatening to some of them. I understood why they would not be willing to help me. I was competition. A lot of these speakers don't have unique stories. They just learned how to be very skilled public speakers.

I wasn't getting much help.

Through trial and error developing a website, social media marketing, e-mail marketing, looking up every webinar and getting the same cliché answers on how to be successful as a motivational speaker, I was a bit frustrated.

This had been the toughest year of my life, transitioning into a new career of being a motivational speaker, all the while being a single dad- A bit like the old Chris Farley skit of the motivational speaker who lives in the van down by the river. (Too close to home, in fact.)

But every morning, I chose to keep getting up. I chose to keep plugging away. I chose to keep walking the talk of being a different breed of speaker. I didn't want to be another "guru" just claiming to be an expert, because I said so.

Yet, I still knew I needed something to help me, and my intuition kept saying I needed to do a TEDx Talk.

Why TEDx Talk?

One: It can give someone prestige and credibility.
Two: It is a "bucket list" experience for many.
Three: It is a glorified business card.

Four: most important for me- It was a full, finished production from A-to-Z, end-to-end, that event planners could sit down and watch an entire production of me speaking in thirteen minutes.

Instead of me sending sizzle reels or clips of a full keynote, someone can now sit down, watch me talk for thirteen minutes and see the full impact of what I'm able to achieve in a completed project.

I knew I needed a TEDx experience on my resume, not only for "bragging rights," but it would make me better as a speaker. It was going to be a challenge. Little did I know how much of a challenge.

I spent hundreds of hours watching dozens and dozens of TEDx Talks, figuring out, or at least trying to figure out what worked and what wasn't working.

And there was some confusion no doubt, as I watched a lot of very good TED Talks, TEDx talks specifically, that were not getting a lot of views. Whereas, there were a lot of TEDx talks, successful ones that had plenty of views, which weren't very good or at least I didn't learn anything new.

With all this information I was researching, I began classifying TEDx Talks into three different veins:

1. Head.
2. Heart.
3. Soul.

*Note: There is a fourth category that I won't spend time analyzing, which is "Comedic Relief." Talks such as "The Orchestra in my Mouth," or "How to Sound Smart in your TEDx Talk," while casual viewer friendly and entertaining, in my opinion, do not do much to serve the spirit of TED.

To break down the three categories-

Head: A TEDx Talk that is well... heady, with scientific facts and leans towards academic lectures. These are often devoid of charisma or emotion.

Heart: A TEDx Talk where you feel the energy, the emotion and passion behind the speaker, but the content isn't really there, or is missing that "something." You don't really learn anything new. "Comedic Relief" can fall under this category.

Soul: A TEDx Talk where you have a speaker who gets up on the stage and speaks from a place of commanding wisdom, authority and vulnerability, from their own personal experiences. They embed themselves into the talk. This is the most important one.

*Note: People remember what they feel, not what they hear. Remember this, **people remember what they feel not what they hear.**

Few TEDx Talks fit exclusively into one category.
Most cover two: Head and heart, heart and soul and head and soul etc.
But rarely do you see someone hit all three. The first person I saw achieve all three, and truly inspired me, was Brene Brown.

She did it brilliantly. That's why her TEDxHouston talk on Vulnerability is one of the most viewed of all time.

It had the <u>Head</u>, with her research, which was fresh knowledge and information that was new to people.

It had <u>Heart</u>, as you could feel her passion as you listened to her speak with such intensity about understanding human behavior.

It had <u>Soul</u>, as you could see how vulnerable she was choosing to be, and the wisdom and clarity she gained through the process, which she was able to convey to all the listeners who have since watched her talk. She embedded herself into the talk.

Brene Brown was able to achieve that trifecta, the God-Head of the Three: Head, Heart and Soul.

This has allowed her talk to become one of the most viewed of all time, and it was a method I wanted to emulate as best I could.

My strategy was now to be break down my talk to make sure it covered all three, effectively:

Head: I wanted to introduce people to a new perspective of polygamy, and educate them on the experiences of young males in polygamy, as the media mostly focuses on the females and young women. I wanted to inform, but also, more importantly, I wanted to challenge my viewers psychologically by flipping it back on them.

Heart: I wanted to bring in heart by showing how I have my own polygamy, how I too was not perfect, and how I deal with it every day, making myself more human to the audience.

For "heart" to be truly effective, I had to do it with engaging passion and humor as well. I knew what I was presenting was heavy stuff, so it was important to introduce a little humor on stage to make my audience laugh and have fun. If I was having fun, then everyone else would be having fun and that would suck people in.

And then there was Soul:

I wanted to tie it all in, and show wisdom through the process I have gained through my own experiences and how I went through life with my own "blinders" on in autopilot mode for far too long. I wanted to establish clarity and be able to articulate it both as a teacher and a guide, to show other people how to escape from their polygamy.

Do your best to try to bring in all three: Head, Heart, and Soul.

Do this and your talk will be very memorable and will have a greater chance of being successful.

Continually ask yourself as you develop and design your talk, if it has:

The Head? The Heart?
The Soul?

If it does, odds are you are going to impact people, and maybe gather a few views along the way.

Which is more important to you? Views or impact? It's a fair question to ask.

If push came to shove, which one would you take, if you could only have one?

My advice- **Go for impact**

Chapter 3
Research Your TEDx Venue and Location

You may have a great idea and an idea worth spreading. But here's a little trick to getting on TEDx stages.

Everyone says they want to talk on "Big" TED, because that's just their ego talking. *Oh, you know I am better than TEDx. My idea is worth being on Big Ted Convention. I'm going to get a "Big TED" invite.*

I liken this hubris and pride to when people say, "I want my son to go to Harvard."

When really, odds are, you're better off going to someplace like the University of Utah, graduating the first in your class at engineering, rather than somewhere where you will be stuck in the middle of the crowd. Statistics show according to Malcolm Gladwell's, *David and Goliath,* that you're better off and more likely to get an amazing job when you go to a smaller school and graduate first in your class rather than getting lost in the pack at an Ivy League School.

The same thing applies to sports.

I have a lot of parents tell me they want their kid to play basketball in the Pac-12 conference or some other big conference. To which I tell them: I don't have any regrets when it comes to my basketball career, but knowing what I know now, if I could do one thing over, I would have gone to Weber State University right out of the gate.

I played two years at the University of Utah, which in 1999 when I signed as a freshman, was considered a perennial powerhouse and Top 10 Program.

At the University of Utah, I was constantly battling for playing time on the bench with other teammates. I was lost in the crowd.

After two years at Utah, I transferred to mid-level Weber State University, where I didn't just get to play but I played all the time.

If you want to be a great basketball player, you have to play basketball, not just practice.

I tell parents this, and I even tell them it is ok to send your kid to a junior college because in this day and age with social media, YouTube and the Internet, if you can play basketball, you will be found.

I've had plenty of teammates that came out of junior college programs, then played somewhere at a mid-level school, and then went off to play in the pros.

If you can play, you'll be found.

This same analogy applies to TEDx versus Big TED.

With the TED structure, Big TED events tend to invite celebrities and people with star power, with the smattering of new voices they pluck from obscurity.

You don't want to be lost in the shadow of "Celebrity."

Whereas, if you can trust the power of the Internet and give a good talk, you will be found.

Here is an important strategy: Many TEDx events, but not all, have what is called "Open Curation."

This is an open call for speakers and submissions.

Therefore, you need to do your research and investigate which TEDx events are open curation.

In theory, while the selection committee may claim to have no preconceived biases or picks, they will have a theme for that year and will be selecting submitted speakers as they see fit to help their theme. While it is open curation and supposed to be 100% objective, it isn't. But still, you have great odds if you believe your idea fits within their theme.

Lucky for me, TEDxSaltLakeCity, the city in which I currently live, was one of these open-curation events. Their theme for 2016 was "Meraki" which translates into, "Passion."

A pretty broad and vague theme. So, I knew their selection criteria might not be as harsh.

Furthermore, the location was a huge play. Not just the TEDx venue and theme itself, but the geographical location and its history of Polygamy with the Mormon Pioneers.

Even better, in the fall of 2015, The Church of Jesus Christ of Latter Day Saints or "Mormon Church" came out with a policy that discriminated against the children of gay people, saying that children of active gay people cannot be baptized into their church. They backed that decision with the justification by saying they've been doing the same thing to children of polygamists.

There was a lot of chaos and tension locally in the Salt Lake City area surrounding this and a lot of people actually turned in their resignation letters to the Church of Jesus Christ.

Why? Because humorously, downtown Salt Lake City itself, Salt Lake City proper, is actually very, very liberal while the rest of Utah is very conservative.

With my background and my story of polygamy, the timing was perfect. I had a great opportunity to share my perspective at TEDxSaltLakeCity, because I knew my audience and I knew the reception and type of people who would be at TEDxSaltLakeCity. I also knew selection committee would be very open to me talking about the Voldemort-esque word of "Polygamy".

Perfect timing.

Now I'm sure some of you are wondering:

"Wait, aren't Mormons polygamists?"
No, they are not. Mainstream Mormons, that is, are not.

Yes, granted, in the early days of the Church of Jesus Christ of Latter Day Saints or the Mormons, the founders of the Mormon faith, Joseph Smith, Brigham Young and company, did in fact, practice polygamy.

Hence, that is why the Mormons migrated out west to Utah to escape religious persecution and practice their religious freedom.

However, as Salt Lake City began to grow and became an interstate commerce hub for the Rocky Mountain West, Utah began to want statehood admission into the United States.

In 1890, the state of Utah agreed to outlaw polygamy in exchange for acceptance into the United States union. From there, many members of the Mormon faith broke away, establishing their own fundamentalist polygamist Mormon sects. Many migrated to Mexico.

Through the years, the LDS Church, or official Mormon church, little by little has become more and more mainstreamed and palatable to the masses, doing its best to avoid speaking of its polygamist past, with many members of the LDS faith unaware of its own history of polygamy.

Now, you can understand when I say: If there's one thing a Mormon doesn't like, it's a polygamist Mormon.

This is because practicing polygamist Mormons are an inconvenient reminder and are disrupting the happy status quo of the Mormon faith, which likes to think they have a perfect history, as any religion does.

Now you see why Polygamy is like the word "Voldemort" to many Mormons and that is why I also knew that the

TEDxSaltLakeCity selection committee would be very interested in having me because it's such a taboo concept.

I knew my venue. It was calculated. It was a foot in the door, to have my story reach millions on the Internet. Instead of needing a home run and trying to get on Big TED, I saw the long game, and knew just like I went in through the back door to the NBA, I could do it again with a TEDx talk.

So, you may have a great idea worth spreading, but you need to figure out the demographic for it. If you love jazz music and have a cool idea worth sharing, you might want to look into Louisiana or Memphis/Tennessee or somewhere around those areas, where there's a niche and strong audience for that.

If it's about wine- TEDxBerkeley or San Francisco is the place to be.

It's all about figuring out the message that you want to share and researching the demographics and locations that your message will most likely connect with. Hit the micro to go macro.

And again, most importantly, look for where it is an open curation. Get on Google, spend time and research.

Know your audience.
Who is offering open call near that audience?

Swallow your pride and aim at speaking to the micro audience at a TEDx venue, with the chance of your talk reaching the macro on the Internet.

Again- Hit the Micro to go Macro.

Chapter 4
Research Your Topic

Do not reinvent the wheel.

A lot of speakers spout the lazy excuse that there is nothing new to be invented or there are no new ideas. Some feel it is just about addressing an idea in a different way, with a different perspective or rephrasing it. I personally feel that's very lazy and that it's also plagiarism.

As a motivational speaker, I see a lot of speakers get up on stage, and basically regurgitate other people's content, without contributing any new content of their own, but because they are very good at public speaking, they make it sound as if it's theirs and make a lot of money doing it.

I made a promise to myself and to my son that if I was going to do this motivational speaking thing that I was going to be producing original content, and not use anyone else's. Heaven knew I had enough different types of experiences that I could share.

Luckily, the TED family demanded this as well.

You don't want to be that guy getting up on a TEDx stage, recycling someone else's ideas and just paraphrasing it. It's awkward and again it's plagiarism.

Why does a student get a failing grade and citation for plagiarism, but speakers do not? Seriously?

Many speakers do this when they get up on the stage, and for those in the crowd who know that they're doing, it is incredibly uncomfortable. It's hard to sit in the audience and listen to someone talk when you know the content isn't theirs. It is totally dishonest, unethical, lazy and ignorant.

If you want to get up on the TEDx stage, you have to research all the TEDx talks that have been presented beforehand. You've got to scour through hundreds of talks, and figure out if your topic has been addressed yet, what has not been covered, or whether your take on a topic that has already been covered has a new twist and is an idea that is worth spreading.

Polygamy being the keyword, it was easy for me to research on the TED forums and YouTube channels. There were only a few talks on it, but nothing near where I was intending to go with it.

It is your responsibility to make sure that your idea is original. Make sure you research because with thousands and thousands of talks, your selection committee will also have to spend time curating all the other talks and submissions and can't fully vet the originality of every talk.

Your job is to make sure that your idea is unique. I have seen a few TEDx talks that bordered on plagiarism of other TED speakers before them. It was embarrassing to watch.

Even if you just want to twist someone else's idea around, you have to be careful.

As I have encouraged you to trust the power of the internet to help you and your idea be found, so too, trust the power of the internet to expose plagiarism. If you plagiarize someone and don't have original ideas, but you so badly want to give a TEDx Talk for your time in the spotlight and bragging rights, you may have your fifteen minutes of fame until everyone figures out that you're just a con artist and a plagiarist.

Question:
Is my topic original?
Did I research it well enough?
Did I really research it?

Chapter 5
Submitting Your Original Idea Worth Spreading

TEDxSaltLakeCity opened their call for submissions in the spring of 2016.

It wasn't until I was in Las Vegas in April of 2016 for an event, that a newly found acquaintance, quickly-turned mentor and confidant, Christoph Merrill, sat me down for a late dinner in a casino.

I was brand new as a speaker. It hadn't been a year yet since my retirement and Christoph heard me at an event the night before.
He was a fan of my authenticity for the five minutes that I spoke. He then spent the time to get online and look at my videos the next day, unbeknownst to me, and called me later that night to sit and have a root beer float following the meal.

It was one of the most influential dinners of my entire life, breaking bread with Christoph. He believed in me. He knew I had something in me.

Yet, when he watched my videos he could tell that I hadn't enough fully unleashed or dug deep down to my potential. He also gave me very important critical feedback when he told me the powerful words,

People don't pay to have you talk about yourself.
They pay to have you help them learn something about themselves.

Christoph had a smile on his face when he said this to me. He said that with corporations and everything, religion is taboo off topic… but that my background of polygamy would make a great topic for a TEDx Talk. We conversed for three hours over many, many things, but most importantly, he believed in me.

It was Christoph who inspired me to finally get off my butt and submit my idea when I returned to Salt Lake City. Even though I still didn't know what the "idea" was quite yet, I had the story, though. That night when I returned home, I got on the Internet and I looked up the TEDxSaltLakeCity website and I then submitted my idea.

I had a five hundred word cap from the submission to share my idea worth spreading:

How does one escape from Polygamy? How does one become aware of inherited thought patterns from such a culture that remain with us, subconsciously that continually damage and sabotage future experiences? As the first legally deaf player in the NBA, dogma and guilt were part of my inheritance. I felt I had to earn love. I was told as a 5-year-old boy in my commune that God had made me deaf as a form of punishment. I carried that chip on my shoulder, thinking that if I made the NBA, God would be proud of me.

As you can see, I was somewhat in the ballpark of "What is Your Polygamy?" But I still had a long way to go. But, I knew I had something in there, within my story, to find an original idea. I just didn't quite know how I was going to make it applicable and generalizable to everyone.

There is a misnomer that people feel they have to have their entire TEDx talk done and completed when they submit. Not true. All you have to have is an idea worth spreading that the selection committee will want to hear more of.

A month later, I got the notification I had been selected to the second round for the final one hundred applicants.

I did a little dance. Now, I needed help. A lot of help. I needed further mentoring.

Chapter 6
Find a Mentor

With the research I began putting into my talk once I was invited to submit a video, I began to understand the successful trend of the combination effect of *Head, Heart, and Soul* as discussed in Chapter 2.

I knew I had a unique opportunity with the background of my story to talk about polygamy, but I also knew that it wasn't enough. I knew I needed something else, a little extra nudge to push through the second round.

It was still only a story, not an idea. I researched TEDx Talks on polygamy and there weren't many of them, a couple of them were pretty dry, and they talked about the finances or polygamy in an abstract concept as far as relationship norms and monogamy, etc.

I knew that I had the platform to give insight into the world of polygamy. But also insight from the male perspective.

Again, we hear all the stories in the media and documentaries about what happens to the young women in polygamy. But you don't really hear about what happens to the men, the young boys growing up.

With that alone, I knew it would be interesting.

But how was I going to flip it?

How was I going to take this very interesting story that people continually ask me about and flip it around to everybody else and make it an "Idea worth spreading."

*Remember: The trademark theme of TED isn't- stories worth sharing.

But rather, ideas worth spreading.

Luckily, I had a friend come into my life named Dennis Allen.

I was sitting with Dennis one day, telling him about my passion for speaking and wanting to be on the TEDx stage.

Dennis is a brilliant executive coach, who through his own free time and interest and passion in my career, sat down with me that day and began brainstorming with me and then he said with a big beaming smile,

"Aha- what is *your* polygamy?"

When he said those words, I smiled too. I saw it.

That simple question was going to allow me to twist and turn it right back on everybody else in the audience and future viewers online.

It was not just going to be me narrating a polygamist experience and informing people about polygamy from a male perspective, but I was going to make it relatable. I was going to make it applicable to everybody else.

That was the idea worth spreading.

I didn't want to be another TEDx Talk lost in the in the crowd.

I was going to make people remember it, because I was going to make them uncomfortable.

Note* People grow and learn when they are just outside their comfort zones.

I was now able to flip it back on everybody else asking them the tough question: what was their polygamy?

People would be uncomfortable, not too uncomfortable, but just enough, and when people are out of their comfort zones, that is when they remember things.

That is when they are challenged and remember the discomfort, as their brain is in new territory, developing new neurological pathways and therefore the memory will remain.

Whereas, if I allowed them to remain comfortable, they weren't going to remember anything. Think about how many times you drive through the same four-way stop sign next to your home? Do you remember every single time you have driven through it? The mundane comfort of routine does not create memories.

Absolutely not.

Whereas, when you take a new detour, you remember those.

I was going to make some people, if not everyone, slightly uncomfortable when I got on that stage; not by insulting them but by challenging them to step outside their comfort zone and do a little self-examination.

It is amazing, the irony of how challenging someone to look inward, is also challenging them to step outward beyond their comfort zone.

I knew that in order for me to do this, and get everyone to trust me as I took them along the path, I had to walk the talk as well. I had to make myself uncomfortable.

Yet, I still would have no idea just how deep this TEDx Talk was going to go.

It's important to have mentors.

I'm not just speaking about the people on the selection committee who are going to mentor you, but finding somebody, whether a paid professional or trusted confidant that isn't afraid to give you blunt feedback.

I have my friend Dennis Allen. He's the one that came up with the question: *What is your polygamy?* Then after that, he and I started brainstorming so many ideas about how we could make this applicable and generalizable for everybody.

We talked for dozens of hours.

Most of the thoughts and ideas we kept coming up with, didn't make it onto the stage. There just wasn't enough time.

But, the fact that we had each other, to bounce ideas off of and the fact that we were comfortable enough with each other, to be honest about what idea was not going to make the cut, was crucial in the genesis of "What is Your Polygamy?"

The fact that we trusted each other and he believed in what I could do, was incredibly stimulating for the emotional and creative process.

You want to find someone that you can bounce ideas off of; sometimes your spouse is good but with your family or spouse, sometimes we don't really know how to give critical feedback without hurting each other's feelings. Literally, too close to home.

That's why I suggest you find a mentor, a professional and just get their advice. Find someone who is well respected in the academic vein of the topic you are researching. Maybe a professor at a nearby university. Find a debate coach.

Find scriptwriters, relationship coaches, someone that you know, or even cold-call them and ask them to be your mentor.

You will be surprised at how many people will be flattered to be asked to be a mentor. Then trust and tell them, *Hey, I have an idea, what do you think about it?*

OK, you like it? How can I make it even more applicable to everyone in the crowd who will be listening to that day and to the potential millions who will be watching it in the future online?

Find someone that you trust but also is not afraid to give you honest feedback. Because like entrepreneurs in capitalistic America, everyone thinks their idea is the best idea and so it is important to have someone bring you down to Earth from time to time, or steer you in a better direction.

Sometimes, you just need to have someone tell you the blunt truth and say, *Ah, it's really not that good, or fresh of an idea. I don't think it'll take.*

Be prepared to receive harsh criticism. It will only make you better.

As a public speaker, I had to sit down many times and receive harsh critical feedback. My instinct every time was to defend myself and retaliate but what has allowed me to grow as quickly as I have, is that I have chosen to welcome all feedback, positive or negative.

I welcome all feedback and then I ask myself how much of it is true? How much of it can make me better? Ask the same with compliments: does it make you better or complacent?

Any criticism that makes you better, is good criticism; whether it's harsh or friendly at the time you receive it.

Get a Mentor.
Continually ask yourself:
Do I simply have a story?
Or is it a new idea?
Be mature enough to receive feedback.
Ask yourself with each compliment or criticism: Is this making me better?
If not, throw it away

Chapter 7
Second Round/Video Submission

The second weekend of May, I received an email where I was notified that I had passed the first round of submissions and these were the guidelines I was given:

Hi Lance,

What an enjoyable process reviewing all the idea submissions for our 2016 event; thank you for sharing yours! We liked it so much, in fact, we're inviting you on to the second round to submit a short video. (You submitted multiple ideas but only one made it to the second round. The text from the submission we're interested in is listed below.)

Think "idea speed dating." Grab a webcam or smartphone and shoot a video of yourself introducing your Big Idea (90 seconds MAX). Tell us your story! Show us your passion! We want our audience to be wowed. Videos longer than 90 seconds will be automatically eliminated from consideration.

At the beginning of your video, please clearly state your name.

Once it's created, share your video with us electronically however you'd like. Upload it to YouTube, Vimeo, use file sharing software to send it to us, whatever you want. (If you need help with the techy side of this, we recommend the Googles. Crazy smart.)

As you create your video, keep in mind that TEDxSaltLakeCity talks 1- are not selling or directly promoting a product or business, 2- have a clearly stated idea, and 3- inspire fresh thinking!

I had 10 days to submit my YouTube video of 90 seconds of my "Idea worth spreading."

But I'm the type of person when I have something to be done like that, I get it done immediately. I don't like letting things stir or simmer. I don't like over-procrastination. With that, I can be a bit overbearing. It comes from 20 years of being a basketball player, playing for coaches and owners that once they make up their mind, they want it done yesterday.

So, with years of conditioning, like Pavlov's dog, I am able to, when demand calls for a sense of urgency, pull rabbits from hats, if not asses. Granted, they aren't always the prettiest rabbits, but they usually pass muster.

I am fortunate in that I am able to conjure up a lot of creativity.

Before I was a baller, I was a creative writer and *Dungeons & Dragons* "Dungeon Master" or DM: Basically, the storyteller and guide.

If I am making it difficult for you to label me, I apologize for not fitting into stereotypes.

I have been called pretty much everything under the sun in my days. And while I am a little bit of everything, I have been called, I am also much more than that. And I am modest to boot!

The Elizabeth Gilbert TED Talk on "Genius" comes to mind when the pressure is on. And genius as the Romans would describe it, comes to me when the pressure is there. I like pressure. I've always enjoyed pressure. As a basketball player, pressure is good; sometimes, but not all the times. But, when the pressure is on and you have to perform in the moment- I've always enjoyed it.

Dennis and I knew we had a really good chance of catching the selection committee off-guard by showing the growth and expansion of the vagueness of my original "idea" submission to now being, *"What is Your Polygamy?"*

Dennis and had I come up with the title, "What is Your Polygamy?" before we even knew we had to submit a video. Dennis was out of town when I received the notice for the video submission, but I knew I had it.

So, I did what I normally do when I need to conjure up creativity... I took a walk. I took a walk in a park for about two hours, recalling and rehearsing what I wanted to say in my 90-minute video clip. I then began to time myself to see how long 90 seconds was. This was because the guidelines were strict: anything longer than 90 seconds, even 91 seconds, was automatically discarded.

Then when I believed I had the right thoughts and the "thread" was clearly visible of where my "idea" was going to go, I turned on my camera phone, right there in the middle of the park, on a rainy Memorial day weekend, and recorded myself, nearly verbatim what you hear me say in the opening segment of my talk:

People often ask me, you grew up in Polygamy? What was that like? I don't get it? Why would people stay? I could never be a second or third wife? That's just creepy?

To which I respond, It's what they know. It's the world they grew up in. And they know what the boundaries and rules are, and they know to stay inside those boundaries at all times, the physical boundaries of the commune and furthermore the mental and emotional boundaries. Stay inside those boundaries and you will always be safe from pain.

So, now I ask you, what is your polygamy? What are the boundaries and thought patterns you have inherited from your childhood? From your parents, grandparents and community that you have taken with you into your adult life? Most people will choose a familiar hell over an unfamiliar heaven.

89 seconds.
Send.

If your selection committee asks you to send a video submission, make sure you have the idea worth spreading, but also at this point, you should know where the "thread" of the presentation is heading.

Chapter 8
Girl Gets Asked to the Dance

The following week after Memorial Day weekend, the TEDxSaltLakeCity team sent me an email announcing that I had been selected to present in September of 2016. I was one of the thirteen.

When I read the email, I did a little victory dance. A little shimmy. I was very excited. I loved the potential that my message was going to reach millions of people but also as a motivational speaker, I knew having a TEDx talk would be huge for my résumé.

The committee asked us to remain silent about the selection, until they did a collective press release on June 20th announcing the speaker lineup. So, I just sat there quietly for three weeks not telling anybody except for Dennis Allen, and of course, he was thrilled for me as well.

But, I would be plenty busy waiting for the announcement as they requested that we submit a rough draft/outline of our talk by June 26th.

Anna Decker was the head curator of TEDxSaltLakeCity and had done most of the correspondence until that point when she handed us off to Jason Shepherd, who was the head speaking coach.

Jason asked me to have the outline presented to him by the end of the month. I was then introduced to Beth Wolfer, who was our team speaking coach, as she would be covering 4 speakers.

I didn't think it would be too hard to get a rough draft submitted.

Little did I know how much this process was going to make me grow, not just as a speaker, but also as a person.

The truth I learned:

A TEDx talk is a journey of self-discovery.

Not a destination.

I had no idea.

I quickly set to work and began hacking out my rough draft of what I wanted to share, the messages and ideas that I wanted to convey to the audience.

Let's just say it was a novel. I did my best to keep in mind, *"18 minutes."*

My very first draft when it was all said and done was 4,500 words.

If you don't know, 4,500 words is a lot of words.

Most humans speak at about one hundred and fifty to two hundred words a minute. So, at that point, I had at best, a 22-minute talk.

And the first rule of TED Talks is *"18 minutes or less."*

Now, some people as you TED fans know, do take liberties with this rule, especially at big TEDx Talks if they have some high status celebrity- They take much more time than is usually allowed. However, I was not one of those, and this wasn't big TED.

Furthermore, my rough draft looked like a schizophrenic wrote it, compared to my final product. I am going to share it with you, so you can see the challenge and growth we made as a team: Jason, Beth and me.

Enjoy reading it... if you can. I cringe.

Chapter 9
Rough Draft

Lance Allred-
TEDx Talk:
Polygamy and Biology of Belief

Being 6'11, I get asked Two Questions on a daily basis, numerous times:

"How tall are you?"

"You played in the NBA with Lebron James, what was that like?"

To which I answer, "I enjoyed it. He's one of the smartest people, not just basketball players, but people I have ever known. And we got along really well, LeBron, the inner city kid from Akron, OH and Me, The Deaf Polygamist Kid."

"You grew up in polygamy? What was that like? Did you see any of the young girls being married off? I just don't get it... Why do people stay? I could never be in a polygamist marriage as a second or third wife. Why would anyone do that?"

"To which I answer, "It's what they know. It's the world they grew up in. It's what they are familiar with. They know what the boundaries and rules are. And they stay inside those boundaries, the physical boundaries of the commune, and furthermore the mental and emotional boundaries, where they have been warned for the longest time, that if they stray too far beyond the boundaries, there is pain. Stay within these boundaries, respect authority and you will always be safe. Safe from pain."

Most people will choose a familiar hell over an unfamiliar heaven.

And now I ask you: "What is your polygamy?"

Now granted, a few of my teammates through the years were practicing their own form of unbridled polygamy, but for the rest of you, truly-

What is your polygamy? What are the boundaries and thought patterns you have inherited from your parents, grandparents, community and culture? What are your comfort zones that you settle in, never daring to take any risk? What is your inner-dialogue regarding your own value and self-worth?

Who here has ever been lead to believe that maybe you aren't quite good enough? That you need to be better? That you had to earn love?

*raise my hand

The greatest con we have ever been sold, is that we have to earn love. People tell us this story to control us. We see this in dogmatic cultures, be it religious or work. The problem with dogma is that it teaches us we have to earn love.
This is the greatest con we have ever been told.
The truth is: Love is either unconditional, or it is not love at all.

I grew up in a world of fantasy, mysticism and wonder. But also of violence,
"My Grandfather, Rulon Allred,"
Show Video Clip. Him speaking. News coverage of his assassination.

I never knew my grandfather as he was assassinated four years before I was born by the wife of a rival polygamist leader, but I was raised in his Utopian dream of Pinesdale, Montana, which he established in the 60s' to escape persecution for his religious beliefs.

It has been scientifically confirmed, from New York's Mount Sinai hospital in 2015, that trauma and beliefs that stem from life altering events are in fact passed down through DNA to further generations. We truly inherit our thought patterns from previous generations. Beliefs are real. They take biological form in our DNA.

Rulon was a victim and martyr for his beliefs. He literally died for them.

My father, the heir to the Rulon's kingdom, was a martyr in that he believed he had to sacrifice all of his hopes and dreams for Rulon's dream. He believed he had to pass on all of his worldly aspirations for treasures in heaven.

I inherited the same victim/martyr complex. At the age of 5, it was impressed upon me by my Sunday school teacher that God had made me deaf as a form of punishment. From the age of 5 until I was 33, I believed I had to earn love and that I wasn't good enough.

Beliefs are powerful, especially when they are handed down through generations.

Quick history lesson for those not aware: Utah as a state, and Mainstream LDS Mormons, do not practice polygamy. Back in 1890, the Mormon/LDS Church outlawed polygamy so that the Utah territory would be able to gain statehood. When that happened, many Mormons broke away and continued to practice the law of polygamy, my grandfather Rulon, being one of them. He was imprisoned in the 40's for practicing polygamy, and when released, he scattered his wives along the Rocky Mountain West, and set up his main haven in Montana, where there were no anti-polygamy laws.

Rulon was a wonderful storyteller and he was able to make people feel safe. We humans are cursed with the quintessential fear of our own mortality. We know we are going to die:

And so, we have beautiful stories to pacify that fear in the form of religion, of how our families will be together for time and all eternity in heaven. It's a beautiful story.

But then you take a big giant needle of steroids and inject it right into the ego and get to believe that not only do you have the "One True Church" but you are also so special. So so special.

That you are God's chosen elite. That your grandfather was a prophet, martyred for his faith and that he is in heaven, on the right hand of God and Jesus, reserving your place there. You are the chosen elite.

It's a drug.

Why would anyone want to let that story go, if they didn't have to? No matter how uncomfortable, abusive, or painful one's situation might be in polygamy, the fear of future pain, of future uncertainty, almost always trumps the reality of the current pain.

People won't change until the pain of their current reality is too great to bear.

So again, I ask you, "What is your polygamy?"

Maybe you hate your job, but you know your paycheck is going to come on the 1st and the 15th. You feel safe knowing it will be there, even though you loathe going to work every morning to your egotistical boss.

Maybe you are in a toxic, abusive relationship and as much as you may dream coming home to your significant other, who makes your life hell, you at least know that someone can stand to be around you, and you just don't know if you put yourself back out there again, if anyone else would want you.

Does the future fear of being alone and single for the rest of your life, trump the current reality of pain and discomfort of an unhappy marriage? Not much different from the unhappy third wife of a polygamist marriage...

As bleak as I am painting this, there are or were good things about polygamy, otherwise, people wouldn't stay. People must always get something out of a situation, or else they wouldn't participate.

Not only do you have the belief that you are so special, which is a drug, you also have the sense of belonging to a community, and being lost in something greater than yourself and it is intoxicating.

As a boy, I could be playing with my 400 first cousins like smurfs in the Montana wilderness, and if I got lost or hurt, there would always be someone there to take care of me, that knew my name...

Everyone knew my name because I was the one with the big giant hearing aides and I talked funny.

The reason why I have 80% hearing loss is due to the RH factor: My mother was RH negative, and my father had RH-positive blood type. Nowadays, it's almost a non-issue with medical advancements, but when you are born in your grandmother's bedroom in a polygamist commune, waiting for Jesus to come again...

I am very lucky to be alive, there is no scientific reason other than:

I simply chose to be alive.

Being the only deaf kid in a 100-mile radius, in Western Montana, there were no amenities to learn sign language. I was thrown into the fire and forced to make do. Even though I loved my cousins and friends, and they loved me, they constantly reminded me that I was not normal, and would still make fun of the way I talked as a boy. It was a competitive world.

I know I speak very well, and most of you won't hear the hearing loss in my language, but I am going to show you a video now, of me at the age of 11. Mind you, I had been in speech therapy for 9 years up to this point, twice a week.

(Show Video)

I have watched this video over 200 times and I still have no idea what the hell I am saying. I am joking, because really, I do, as this is what people sound like to me. Deaf people talk this way, from the back of our mouths, so that it vibrates through our skull so we feel like we are making a sound and you can then hear us.

In the media, we often hear the harrowing stories of the women and young girls who are married off to older men, rightfully so, but we don't hear much of the impact it has on the lives of the boys who grow up in that world.

Again, it was competitive because you saw men in power, the prophets, with multiple wives. And so as a boy, you begin to equate women as a way of showing your worth as a man. More wives=more worth=more power. This was a logical conclusion for a 5-year-old boy.

And also, the women didn't need what we called, "The Priesthood," the spirit blessing that allows men to receive revelation from God. The reasoning was that women already are so inherently pure, that they don't need the priesthood.

A clever logic twist to control women no doubt, but as a boy, you see it as God and women will define your worth, your manliness, to provide as a father and husband, and also to commune with God.

Of course, from a perspective, this was incredibly objectifying of women. Polygamist men can go one of two ways: some chauvinistic men who regard women as property, and then you have men who put women on pedestals.

I grew up in a monogamous home, where my father was the theologian and scholar of the Allred group. And he was loved. Everyone expected my father to be the heir to Rulon's throne. But he could not, unless he married a second wife. So, in a twisted way, because my father did not practice polygamy, we as a family, were not quite "good enough."

Can you imagine how competitive that world was? Once a girl began to blossom as a teenager, not only did you like her, but your brother liked her, your 200 male cousins, not to mention the large broods from other clans, even your uncles, heck, even your dad is your competition!

This is why many polygamy clans cull their male population and banish them when they turn into teenagers, creating the "Lost Boys" effect. It was a way to lessen the competition.

This is a dialogue I had on a certain day when I was a kid, "Steven Don" I asked, because with that many cousins, you always have to use a middle name to clarify which Steven you are speaking to. "I think I really like Lisa. Do you think she might like me back?"

"No."

"Why not?"

"Because I already claimed her. I called dibs."

"But you called dibs on Sarah…"

"Yeah so… We're polygamists…"

"Ok…"

By now you are seeing why as a boy, I developed the thought pattern and tendency to put women on pedestals, that they were where I was going to find my self-worth, my value. That I had to earn their love, because they were inherently better than me!

I was terrified of girls. I was already shy about they way I sounded and I was afraid of not hearing them correctly, so I avoided interacting with them well past high school. If they rejected me, what did it say about me and my worth?

At the age of the 13, my father had discovered that several of our religious leaders, or prophets, had been abusing their children for years. And we were like, "If these are men of God, how is this even possible?"

We knew it was a lie and my father announced he would no longer be attending. People were angry, not angry at our so-called prophets who were abusing their children, but angry at my father for rattling the paradigm and shaking their belief that we were the true faith. That we were special.

Belief is a very powerful thing. The nature and appeal of beliefs is that they provide "certainty," in an uncertain world. They are absolutes.

And most people want to view our otherwise very complex world through a black and white lens. Life is much easier to process and handle through such a scope, especially when the scope tells you that you are special, that you are right and that you have the "truth."

In the world of absolutes that is polygamy, there are lots of ironies and dichotomies such as:

On one hand- You are so so special. And yet on the other... you are not worthy enough. If you become disenfranchised in polygamy or unhappy or something bad happens, "Oh you weren't committed enough. The lord is withholding his blessings because you didn't follow the exact formula. The prophet is never wrong. All you had to do was listen to the prophet, pray harder and have more faith."

And here is another dichotomy: You are loved unconditionally by God, without measure, without question... on the condition that you do everything the prophet says...

Even as kids, you experience these dichotomies: you are told lying is a sin. You will not be able to go to heaven as God will be angry with you, but then you are also told that if anyone asks where you come from or if your Dad is a polygamist that you should lie.

It should come as no surprise that with these polarizing games of mental gymnastics, there is a lot of mental illness in polygamy. I wish I had a scientific study to show you to back up this statement, but its kind of hard to round up a bunch paranoid, gun-toting, libertarian conspiracy-theorist polygamist to talk about their feelings for a scientific study to confirm this... so you just have to take me at my word when I say, especially in my Allred gene pool, there is a tremendous amount of bipolar disorder, schizophrenia, anxiety/depression, suicide and OCD (which I have suffered from).

When we left the Allred Group, we had to go into hiding. We were the only ones that left the group. My Dad's siblings, polygamist or monogamous, could not let go of the idea that they were special, and that my grandfather, Rulon, was the prophet. It was such a part of their identity.

As it was for me!

Apart from losing my cousins and best friends, the hardest part about leaving the Allred group was losing my identity as the special kid. At least I had that going for me. But now, I wasn't anymore... I no longer had the certainty I was so used to. I was not living in an unfamiliar world, a world of the unknown. And I have remained in that world ever since, a challenger of the unknown.

After a time, we eventually settled in Downtown Salt Lake, when I began 8th grade. I grew 6 inches taller that year, from 5'10 -6'4. I slept a lot. And I had never played organized basketball before that point. I was clumsy, uncoordinated, and my inner imbalance was atrocious.

The basketball coach saw me walking down the hall one day and said, "You should come try out for the team."

Sure, I thought. It will be a good way to find friends.

I wasn't very good at first.

But I had that chip on my shoulder, of people always telling me what I could and couldn't do. They said I couldn't play basketball with my hearing aides due to sweat and concussion issues.

The greatest challenge of a physical disability is not the initial disability itself, it's the limitations the people around you place on you, and the limitations you place on yourself, if you believe them.

So, what is your disability? We all have them. What are the limitations you have allowed yourself to believe exist, that have now for many of you become an excuse to stay within your comfort zone?

But I never had a comfort zone. Every morning I put my hearing-aids on, I am pushing myself beyond them. More often than not, when I wake up, I hated putting my hearing-aids on. But I was not here to stay within my comfort zones. That is not what I am here on this Earth to do. I am here to communicate.

All of my life, people have been telling me what I can and cannot do, I just simply chose not to listen. I can't hear them very well anyway. When I was in polygamy and shortly after we left as well. When I started playing basketball, even the limitations piled on. "You're too deaf to play, you can't even hear the whistle. You're too clumsy."

I simply choose not to listen, because I can't hear them very well anyway.

I have a nasty habit of proving people wrong.

But also, even though we had physically broken away from polygamy, that was the easy part. Escaping polygamy mentally, emotionally? That is the hard part.

While I cognitively knew as a teenager developing critical thought, that polygamy was a lie, deep in my subconscious, I still believed that I wasn't enough, that I had to be better, that I had to earn love.

I still had a warped concept of God.

And deep in my mind, those old beliefs still lingered and matured with me, as I believed I had to become the first deaf player in NBA history and then God would finally be proud of me. And then not only would he love me, but then I would be worthy of love from other people.

As a 14-year-old kid, the pressure I placed on myself to be perfect was intense. Every made or missed shot had eternal ramifications.

There is a common pattern seen in people escaping polygamy. While they take the pain to physically escape and step out into the unknown, they will rarely take the even more painful step of mentally escaping polygamy. They will never fully step out beyond their comfort zones, and more often than not, will return to polygamy; or gravitate to other ex-polygamists where they settle in a cushy co-dependent comfort zone, something akin to the environment where they grew up.

And now, we as a family were choosing to break the chain. We chose this.

And it was hard and painful.

The problem with emotional health is that there is no real criteria for it. It is an abstract concept, which is hard to compute, especially for ex-polygamists like us who come from a world of blind absolutes.

But for all the linear thinkers out there, I will take a crack at it and share with you how I define emotional and mental health, by questions that I ask myself every day:

Do I hold myself accountable for not only my thoughts and actions, but for my reality?

Do I catch myself processing information and immediately assuming guilt or shame, like the polygamist Mormon I was? Do I catch myself wanting to deal and think in absolutes, that I have absolute "truth?"

I ask these questions because another common path you see polygamists take when they escape is that they turn atheist, raging that: *Not only was Joseph Smith, the founder of Mormonism a fraud, but they claim that God doesn't even exist. There is no God! Let's throw the baby out with the bathwater!"*

They take their same degree of conviction and flip it into a new paradigm. They go from one extreme absolute to the other.

They were right before, but now they're really right!

When I listen to a former a Mormon explain why God does not exist, I hear the words they are saying, but I am listening deeper at the pattern of thought with which they are voicing their absolute stance... and you know what they sound like? They sound like an angry Mormon.

Basketball was also a nice buffer, because not only did I carry with my thought process about God, but I still had the same anxiety about women. I didn't date in high school because I was pretending to be so focused on basketball that I didn't have the time, which was partly true, but also an excuse because I so feared being rejected by a woman.

These old thought patterns and biological beliefs would hamper and trip me up for many years. They were a double-edged sword, as they drove me to insatiable work ethic, but also recurring clashes with coaches and authoritarian figures who abused their power and engaged in double standards. When you grow up in a black and white world of absolutes, nothing pushes your buttons like double standards and hypocrites.

Flash forward to 2008, when I am 27 years old after a rocky college career and shoddy experiences toiling over in Europe, and I do in fact become the first legally deaf player in NBA history when I am called up to the Cleveland Cavaliers. It was a great day.

It was an amazing experience to be able to stand there on the court, in a place where so many told me I would never be able to go.

I had chosen to do something that people said was crazy. And I did it.

But then one game, when I was shooting a free throw in Cleveland, OH at Quicken Loans arena, a thought came into my head, and it was so silent that it was deafening, "Is this it? Is this the best that it gets? Why don't I feel any different? Why don't I feel that God loves me any differently than before?"

I had been chasing that Hollywood myth of a happy ending.

The paradigm that was my reality, began to crumble. Severe depression and near suicide followed.

But I choose clarity. I choose to break the cycle and learn the lessons.

The painful lesson being: the stories we tell ourselves which we believe are real.

I am not smart.

I am not pretty.

I am too fat.

I have to earn love.

We hold onto these stories like a hot coal in our hands, no matter how badly it burns, because we believe, like some sort of merit badge that they are our identity, that they have value, and that they somehow define us.

But, they are only stories. Stories that we make incredibly powerful when we enable them to morph into beliefs.

I no longer choose old stories that no longer serve me. I choose clarity. And the greatest clarity came when my son was born.

When I held him for the first time, I finally understood what unconditional love was. It was something I had never allowed myself to feel.

And in that moment, I finally got it. "I get it. This is love."

For years, I had believed love was to be earned, and that it come from some outward source.

This belief was so powerful that I traveled the continents, thinking that next job, that next car, that next lover, my spouse, that NBA contract on the biggest stage in the world, would heal that wound and close that hole in my heart.

Guys, not even the brightest lights in the world, that NBA stage, could heal that void.

Only I could. Granted, with the help of my son. But only I truly could.

And I have chosen to break the cycle of these biological beliefs, for I do not wish to pass them on to my son. He deserves better, far better than to inherit these old patterns and beliefs that no longer serve me. My son will know, through me, that his worth is immeasurable.

Don't be like me, going on some Alchemist's journey for 10 years around the world, trying to find your validation and worth through the eyes of others or the outcomes of life.

Choose Clarity.

Choose to be leaders of your own lives.

Choose to be lions.

And again, most importantly, above all else, if you must have an absolute in life, Choose this one:

Love is either unconditional, or it is not love at all.

Thank you.

Chapter 10
Hubris

I thought I would get eighteen minutes, maybe even more than eighteen minutes… At least I was planning on 18 minutes. I even went as far as to try and big time Jason and Beth with an email note I sent along with the first draft saying to trust me with 18 minutes, or maybe even allow me to go over, (because I was somehow really important, right?) and I had the right connections with the media and elsewhere to make the video do well.

Hubris and Ego.

Ugh, I roll my eyes at myself more than anyone else could possibly ever know. It was pretentious.

And luckily, Jason Shepherd did not back down.

And I am so grateful looking back, I didn't go for 18 minutes. People really do have the shortest attention span these days. Truly.

I get a smile on my face looking back, thinking that I was important enough that they should somehow bend the rules for me and allow me to have more than 18 minutes.

In total, I gave Jason and Beth over twelve drafts. We continually went back to the drawing board. I met with them in person over four times, and with emails and communications being overlapped in between.

I would send them a new draft but before they could even respond, I had already sent them another one. I think they hated me at some point; maybe even wanted me banished to Tangiers.

And I couldn't blame them- who wants to work with a neurotic, pretentious diva?

The biggest pain we had is that we kept miscommunicating on how many stories and anecdotes and at what age of my timeline they wanted those anecdotes.

I wasn't sure if they wanted more stories on polygamy, or how was I going to make it applicable to everybody. Did they want more experiences in polygamy, or did they want more aftermath clarity?

I kept misinterpreting, I kept going back and giving them a new draft.

"This one has too many stories, we want more insight."

"Lance, we want the actual application of the knowledge and lessons to be learned. How does it relate to us?"

Then, *"Oh, well actually you took out too many stories. Can you put some stories back in?"*

And so on.

It was a very frustrating and painful process for us.

It recalled to mind the movie, *A River Runs Through It,* when Norman MacLean's father was homeschooling him and kept sending his paper back with red markings, "Again, half as long."

And I would sulk off.

Here is the important thing:

Every time I communicated with them, and every time they sent me back with my latest draft, I never argued with or challenged them. At first, with the pretentious email I came out of the gate with, I am sure they feared I would be difficult to work with.

But, I did my best to never challenge them or be defensive.

I never said they didn't know anything. I simply listened to them. And I welcomed their feedback. I could have easily said, "I am a paid public speaker, what do you know?"

But I didn't

That was not easy to do, because I was pouring my heart and soul into the text. It was personal.

And you know what?

This process and experience made me twice the speaker that I was before. It taught me the power of brevity.

Brevity is the soul wit.

It taught me that less is indeed more. It taught me to stay focused and not go off on long tangents anymore, or at least far fewer ones than I did before. It taught me the power of connecting with people through the stories hidden between the lines.

Furthermore, Jason and Beth challenging me, made me keep digging and digging deeper into the project, to a place I didn't want to go emotionally. But, that is where I had to go, and whether they consciously knew it or not, and I like to think they did, they made me go there. I like to think they knew I had something else, far deeper.

I am pretty sure I submitted the most drafts, if not more, than all the other 12 speakers combined.

Welcome the feedback.

Submit your draft to the speaker's committee multiple, multiple times. And have the humility to listen to their feedback, even if they are dead-wrong on an idea. Listen.

Always welcome feedback. If you don't agree completely, after everything has been said, there's always one or two things that surely you can take and apply and make the speech even better.

Chapter 11
Denial

I kept submitting all these drafts asking: *What is your polygamy?*

Yet, I wasn't truly asking myself, *what is mine?*

My divorce had been finalized in March of that year, 2016, just a few months prior.

Simon's mother and I split in the fall 2014 and I had to finish off that last season without my son. It was the most painful thing I had ever experienced.

The only way to cope was to go into autopilot mode and focus on finishing my career. If I had dealt with the emotions then, I would have surely collapsed.

In order to survive, I felt nothing and focused strictly on basketball. And then when I retired and returned home, I didn't really have a clear plan. I said *"Oh, I have to start working. I have to make money. I got to get a new job and be able to support my son. Otherwise, I have to keep playing basketball and I do not want to do that. I know! Let's become a public speaker! People ask me to speak all the time for free. Maybe I can get paid to do it!"*

Work became a very convenient distraction and that I didn't have to worry about any emotions regarding my failed marriage or the loss of love, all I had to do was focus on work.

A motivational speaker in denial of his own feelings-sounds ironic, right?

But you would be surprised at how par for the course it is.

Spending hundreds of hours studying past speakers, watching YouTube videos of successful talks, TEDx Talks and also motivational public speakers, I began hashing out all those details figuring out what works, what doesn't, while finding and maintaining my authentic voice- Or so I thought, was my authentic voice.

And this distraction worked for a while, as I pretended I was above all such nonsense of human emotions, sadness, grief and loss, because, *Hey, I was a motivational speaker! I was a paragon of emotional health! I shouldn't feel anything. Nothing. Feelings are for lowly humans. I am a superhero! There is only happy and positive!*

My mentality for years was, *"Buck up!"* or *"Find the silver lining."* It's what I had to do all my years as a professional basketball player, with all the frustrations of my pro career dealing with teams who didn't pay or went bankrupt.

It was my coping mechanism, to find the silver lining and say, *"Oh well, on to the next experience, and at least I have my health or at least I got some of the money…"*

While I had lots of anger and frustration boiling beneath the surface as a pro basketballer, my only coping skill was to stonewall and not address it and not focus too much on the anger and frustration because it was always about the next job, or the next game.

If you add up the money I am owed around the world as a pro-baller, from contracts signed that were never honored, it is about $900,000. Yep…

However, as a basketball player, if I had spent too much time being angry with the team or past teams, I would be an ineffective player in the moment, in the game, when my job was on the line.

I learned to be a sentry, a soldier with no emotions.

And this is what I did when my ex-wife left with our son. I simply chose to focus on basketball. I didn't feel any emotions. I was a gladiator. And I naively carried that same mentality into being a public speaker.

This is why I didn't feel I was a developing as fast I felt I should have with my story and knowledge and experiences around the world. This is because I wasn't walking the talk.

Rather, I was being a charlatan. I was becoming something I swore I would never become.

Sure, I had my own original content. But I was telling people how to heal their lives, how to be leaders of their own lives, and I wasn't doing the same.

I had not taken the time to actually address the grief and the loss of my marriage.

During that summer of 2016, as I was working on my TEDx Talk, I was asking myself constantly, *"What is your polygamy?"* and how I could make it applicable for other people. I kept missing the mark.

It was flat. Flat meaning, it was good, sure, but Jason and Beth knew there was something else there.

In those drafts, I was bringing up many scenarios of what people might do and how that could be construed as their polygamy and using past experiences, but I was avoiding. I was in denial.

At the time of this process, my son, Simon, was about to turn three and it was time to get him enrolled in a preschool.

Consequently, I had to do much more correspondence with my ex-wife and I did not realize how much I had suppressed my grief and anger, because eventually a lot of that anger was being directed at her. A lot of anger. Hurtful e-mails and hurtful words were exchanged.

And yet here I was being a motivational speaker. Really?
That's not really walking the talk.

That summer I came to the realization of what my polygamy was:

How I still believed I had to earn love. That I had to be a superhero. That the five-year-old kid in me, who was told that God had made him deaf as punishment, still believed that he had to be perfect. That he had to play in the NBA, that he had to have the perfect marriage, that he had to be validated by the love of a woman.

I needed to believe that my wife was perfect, that our marriage was perfect. So that would mean that I was a good man.

If there was a disagreement, I didn't know how to argue, because my parents never argued. They had disagreements but there was never an argument, ever.

I didn't know how to have an argument or a disagreement. My only coping skill was to stonewall, to simply shut down and not talk about it. I had no skills in that area; even after all the years of playing basketball- I avoided conflict.

I did whatever I could to end an argument even if it meant just saying, "Ok, you're right," even if I didn't really mean it.

I could see how this would have been very frustrating for my ex. And also how frustrating it was for me to put her on a pedestal- Needing her to be happy, so that would mean I was a good man. How smothering and claustrophobic that must have been for her.

This is when the TEDx talk became something greater.

I thought it was just going to be me getting on a stage, talking about a cool idea, being a "thought leader." I supposedly thought I would simply be showing how well-spoken I was and how talented I was as a public speaker and ride off into the sunset with plaques and airborne kisses sent my way.

My story was going to undergo metamorphosis. When at first I had expected it to be about Polygamy, *"What is your Polygamy?"* became more about me going through, and coming out of the grieving cycle.

I did not know how to grieve.

My childhood growing up in polygamy, all I knew how to do was be happy, peaceful and content. Because any other emotions were bad, ungrateful or evil.

The old narrative was, if I was sad or frustrated, it meant that I was not grateful for the blessings that I had. I was not grateful just to be here on this earth. I was not grateful to God.

I was taught as a boy, in my culture, that you do not express emotions. I didn't know the first thing about grief, or how to grieve.

51

What was my polygamy?

I didn't know how to feel. I didn't know to cope with emotions that weren't the emotions of peace and happiness.
Anger? Grief? Bad!
I was stunted emotionally.
I still believed I had to earn love.

Ask yourself this question: How are you going to be more real and genuine with your audience when you get on the stage?
How are you going to connect?
How are you going to show your humanity?
How will you make sure they remember you?
Are you going to be bold?

Chapter 12
Your Peeps

Get to know your fellow speakers, not just the selection committee and the speaking coaches.

TEDxSaltLakeCity selection committee did a fun thing for us, when they had a Saturday morning planned out in August where the speakers would all get together and present their ideas and also practice the first minute of their talk and also the most powerful minutes of their talk.

We had two good speaking coaches that day who had been part of TEDx events before, as well as the entire selection committee in attendance. This was my very first time meeting everyone. I had only met Beth and Jason and the other speaking coaches before this point, while submitting my many, many drafts.

This was going to be my first time actually getting up and presenting it in front of a crowd. But it wasn't just any crowd, it was my peers and there were only twenty people in the room.

Take it from me- It's far easier to speak to five thousand people than it is to speak to twenty people.

It is a strange thing but when there's a mass audience watching you, it is not nearly as personal. Just like it is easier to speak for 50 minutes than it is for 5, it is easier to speak to a large crowd than a small one.

But I truly enjoyed this process of speaking in front of them; it was great practice. They were my coaches and my fellow speakers who were going to be presenting their own projects and so, therefore, they were going to give me feedback.

Granted, it was uncomfortable and unnerving, because when I speak in public as a professional, I just talk for an hour. They then give me an ovation and I walk away and maybe sign some books. But on this practice day, I had to stand there for minutes after I presented and just receive feedback. Being critiqued one-on-one is petty compared to being critiqued in front of an audience. But that is where growth happens- outside your comfort zone.

I'm grateful I did because it gave me ideas, lots more ideas about what I could do. I got great body language coaching from the coaches there about how to shift around a little bit when demonstrating a dialogue.

But here's the thing, I am not much for when people are coaching you about technical things like body language or posture. I never did Toastmasters or other speaker training. It is too "robotic" for me, and disingenuous when you can tell people have rehearsed their body language. Some people enjoy that, but I don't, because at the end of the day, you still have to be you.

When there's someone telling you what to do with your hands all the time, and then you are more focused on what you are doing with your hands, you are in your head and not present. You're speaking from your head and not your heart.

Be you. Always be yourself when on the stage. Always speak from your heart.

Don't worry about your posture this or that. Posture comes with confidence, which comes with the repetition of getting up on stage and being comfortable talking in front of people.

Sure, you can go to Toastmasters and you can be a little more conscientious of your body and what you're doing. But again, if you are spending too much time in that head, you're not speaking from your heart and my motto throughout this book will always be: people remember what they feel, not what they hear.

Hopefully, your TEDx committee has events like this for you to meet your peers and present your ideas back and forth to each other.

I loved the experience of not only getting feedback from my peers but being able to help and connect with them as well.

I could see some of them who had very little experience in public speaking and but they had ideas they really wanted to share and I liked their ideas.

I was more than happy to submit or give them my opinion on what they could do when they get on stage.

I didn't ever bother to coach them about what to do with their hands or their stance. I just told them as I tell you now, always stand in your authentic space.

Always be in your authentic space.

Don't try to be anyone else- Just be you. Be your authentic self, always.

You cannot fail when you do.

Should your TEDx event not be organizing these sorts of team get-togethers with your fellow speakers, I strongly suggest you take the time to reach out to those who are speaking with and establish relationships with them. Meet them for lunch, maybe organize your own team get-together.

I strongly encourage it. If you're the only one of your TEDx team who is reading this book, organize a group meeting, get all the other speakers together. Help each other out. I understand the initial reaction is to think of them as maybe your competition.

I was worried too, the day I showed up. It's human nature to see all the other speakers and think that you're in a competition.

Who's going to be selected to speak when? Who's going to be the opening? Who's going to do the closing? Who's going to be in the prime time? Who's going to get the most views? Who does the selection committee like better?

All those thoughts are going to come into your head and that's completely normal. You're human.

As a motivational speaker, I tell everyone the whole "New Age" thing borders on BS most of the time. All that rabble about permanently rising above the "Ego."

That's not real life. We're human and the ego has its use: the ego calls for competition and improvement. It calls for self-development. Yet, it is a two-edged sword in that it is also self-destructive and when not used correctly, gets us into most of our problems.

But just as the ego is what drives violence, it is also drives us humans for a better world. Competition is good. I am very competitive. It's true.

I look at other public and motivational speakers and I immediately want to know their story. Do they have a real platform, experiences that are out of the ordinary, or are they just really upbeat and positive?

The latter don't inspire me at all, because anyone can regurgitate other speakers and be really positive. That is my ego and that is my being competitive, and it is also what drives me to get better and better.

If you didn't have an ego, you wouldn't be reading this book. It is the ego within you that inspired you to submit your idea. It is the ego within you, inspiring you to get up on the TEDx stage and share your idea with others. It is the ego.

You might want to hear yourself say, *it's the spirit, or God* or whatever and that might be part of it. I'll give you that.

But the ego is involved as well- let's not kid ourselves.

Your ego is very excited about the idea of receiving a standing ovation for your brilliant original idea and that is okay. That is what makes us human.

Take the time to get to know your TEDx team of fellow speakers. Bond with them. Connect with them. When you do you will be happy for their success and that energy will be contagious and palpable like it was for us at TEDxSaltLakeCity 2016.

Chapter 13
Method

A lot of people have asked me, *"Did you write your entire talk out? Did you memorize it? Did you just use notes and have an outline of what you're going to talk about?"*

Originally, I thought I was just going to do an outline, but the more and more I thought about it, I realized I had just ten to fifteen minutes to have an impact.

As a speaker, if you tell me that I have an hour to give a keynote, I do very little planning. I find out people's pain points when I speak with that company beforehand, and then I quickly, within a day or so, gather the stories that I know will have the best impact to share. And then I have an outline, solidified by videos or other things in my keynote presentation to help me guide myself, and the audience through the presentation.

I have done it enough times that I'm actually very good at it now. I need very little prep work when I'm being told that I have an hour because I know I have time to go through the stories and explore tangents if I feel the inclination as I read the audience's body language.

It is fun being a keynote speaker and having the liberty to improvise and be in the moment.

Again, people remember what they feel not what they hear. And so, if they're connected with me emotionally because they can tell that I'm actually talking to them, not just preaching to them, but talking and engaging with them, they're going to remember those things.

Yet, if someone tells me I have only have thirty minutes, it means I got some work to do. I got to figure out what stories have to be edited, made more concise, or even entirely redacted. Rather, I have to be more selective in what stories to

57

use that will be most efficient and impactful with the time that I'm given.

Now, imagine my surprise when TEDxSaltLakeCity told me that I had ten to thirteen minutes.

Oh boy.

I have so many stories and experiences about polygamy that I did not have the time to share.

If you give me the room for an hour, I'll tell you so many stories about polygamy and lessons learned. But thirteen minutes? Yeah, this was going to be a challenge.

My original naiveté said that all I have to do is just have an outline. *"I can make that work and I'll do well because it will be on the fly and I won't sound rehearsed."*

I thought I could pull it off.

Yet, whenever I timed myself at home, it was awful. It was a train wreck. I would ramble, get lost, then panic as I couldn't remember which idea I was about to bring up, or forgot to bring up because I explored a tangent.

The last thing you want to do is ramble.

Because you only have so much time and who knows? A TEDx stage may be the only time you ever get the opportunity to really stand in front of a stage and impact large masses.

Knowing this may be your only shot, you need to make every word count.

Even though my career is as a speaker and I knew I would always have other opportunities in the future to share my wacky story, I knew the TEDx stage was an entirely different and unique opportunity.

I knew that if it went well, not only would I impact the people in the room that day at TEDxSaltLakeCity, but potentially millions on the Internet following that event. I knew I needed to make every word count.

My plan was to then write the script.

Write the script yourself. Yes, you can have people help but you need to be the main contributor.

People ask me if someone else wrote the script for me.

No, it was me.

I had Dennis helping me with some ideas. Dennis and I had a lot of ideas. Most of them, ninety percent of them did not make the cut.

And it was hard.

With Jason and Beth giving me constant feedback, going back and forth the drawing board, my final draft, turned out to be 1,300 words.

That's quite a cut from 4,500 words in the first draft.

So, there's an expression which is very important for you to remember. Chris Anderson, head curator of TED even says it and was the most helpful bit of advice I took from his book when he said,

"Kill Your Darlings."

It's hard to do because you have so many sentimental and powerful stories that you think will help people. I know it hurts. But you have to.

You simply don't have enough time.

Sorry. It's the truth. You have to kill your darlings and figure out which stories, which points you can make that will have the broadest impact possible.

I know you're probably like me in that you think if only...

If only I can quickly share all the points I want to, I will be able to have a broader impact and make everyone like it!

It won't happen. I'm sorry. You only have so much time.

And news flash: those that are going to dislike you, will dislike you anyway; no amount of extra points or clarifications or efforts to make everyone feel welcome or see the point of the talk will make a difference.

Haters are gonna hate.

I've had many people criticize my talk over points, or lack thereof, that I would have made if I had had more time and they would have seen, had I had more time.

If only I could have shown them my original drafts.

They attack my story for some holes or flaws that were covered in the original drafts, but did not make the cut, and of course part of you wants to defend yourself. But, that's the price you pay if you want to get up on the TEDx stage: You're making yourself public and you have to be ready for criticism and for feedback and it's going to hurt.

Welcome to the world of public life.

But, if you want everyone to like you, remember:

Say nothing, do nothing, be nothing.

But that is the exact opposite of what you are doing by getting on the TEDx stage.

Haters are going to be all up in your grill now.

As you prepare and work on your drafts, remember: Kill your darlings.

You don't want anything more than fifteen hundred words, that is my personal opinion. Anything more than that and you'll be talking way too fast.

The average person again speaks from 150 to 200 words per minute. Remember this. If you talk at more than 200 words, you will sound like Alvin and the Chipmunks.

And people are going to remember what they felt, which was annoyance.

Big suggestion: Start recording yourself on your phone.

I began recording myself on my phone when I got it down to 1,500 words, somewhere in the twelfth draft. This is a brilliant thing to do. Record yourself on your phone and then listen to the playback.

You're going to hear the "dead spots" in your talk, which are where you begin to get bored every time you listen to your talk and will want to fast forward or begin daydreaming and stop following along.

When you find yourself getting bored, that's a cue to take out that segment from your talk.

Because if you're getting bored, trust me, the audience will be getting bored.

You're going to hear sentences, syntaxes and structures that sound good on paper, that just do not sound good when you're speaking publicly.

This is one of the strongest of pieces of advice I can give:

Record yourself on your phone, save the file and listen to the feedback.

Over and over, and over again.

I did this hundreds of times.

Not only did I listen to my feedback hundreds of times, I probably made twenty plus different recordings, new drafts, new additions on top of additions.

I listened to them dozens of times while I was taking walks and while I did, I'd have the script in my hand and ink out or add notes on the script that came to me as I listened to the playback.

Notice what expressions just don't work. While they may work on paper, they may not work in public speaking.

You will be inspired by all the many ideas that come to you when you allow yourself to critique your own speech, listening to the playback.

If you have a good balance and grip on reality, you're going to make yourself better. You're going to be your own greatest critic. And you will push yourself more than anyone else possibly can.

Chapter 14
Pilgrimage

Leading up to your TEDx event, find the time to take a vacation for yourself; nobody else.

And it's not a vacation, it is a sabbatical. It is a pilgrimage. Research and find some place in nature that is considered by many to be a holy or spiritual place. I don't mean a church, Vatican, or Buddhist temple. I mean nature.

There are places in nature that the native people in any country consider spiritual and sacred.

Having been born in Montana, and raised near Glacier National Park, I know what beauty is. I have traveled to many wonderful places yet, there is one place I've never been and that was the Redwoods in California.

I have always aimed to visit those forests and knew it was something I've always needed to do but I've never been. And it kept calling my name.

I have spent a lot of time on the Oregon coast. The Oregon coast is my end-game but I've never spent time on the Northern California coast.

In the final month leading up to TEDxSaltLakeCity, I was about near my wit's end. I needed to get out of town. And you will feel the same.

I figured it was time for a pilgrimage. I got in my single-dad minivan, my Toyota Sienna and figured, *You know what? I am going to do this whole California dreamin' coast thing and live out of my van for five days.*

My son was going to be with his mother for a five-day weekend, so I planned around that time to get in my car and drive from Salt Lake City through the desolate and forgettable Nevada desert, up through Northern California until I hit the Redwoods. Sorry, Nevada... you really are forgettable.

Google maps lied to me when they said it would be a thirteen-hour drive. It ended up being an eighteen-hour drive. While I was in the car for all those eighteen hours, that's when I turned on the audio books and listened to Chris Anderson's book and I also listened to Malcolm Gladwell's, *David and Goliath*.

I have awesome headphones, and I also have to blast everything at full volume, in case you were wondering how I hear audiobooks. Even then they can be frustrating when they hire the readers with soft voices.

Often times, I can't listen to podcasts or audiobooks, because they do produce them at such low volumes.

This is actually why I don't listen to podcasts... they are infuriating with how low a volume/amplitude most people record them at... not to mention how many people with mousy voices think they have a good radio voice, when in fact, they do not.

Wait, you are an inspirational speaker and you don't listen to podcasts?

Nope, no I don't. It is a struggle to listen to them. It's not because I think I am too good to learn anything new. But, it does feel like everyone and their mother has a podcast about "how to be successful."

Luckily, these two books, *David and Goliath and The Official TED Guide to Public Speaking*, were at adequate volume production.

I don't always hear everything, but I can catch up pretty well and fill in the gaps. And when you are driving for that long, there is plenty of time to fill in the gaps.

Find awesome audio books that inspire you and spark outside-the-box thinking.

Not just books about how to make more money or be a successful entrepreneur. But find books that inspire you and educate you about the human psychology and the way people think and what makes them tick. Find books that challenge your own perception of truth.

You have to learn about people if you're going to be a public speaker because in many ways you actually become a human sociologist or psychologist, even if not a professionally certified.

Nonetheless, you're dealing with human emotions and psychology. You're learning about what makes people tick and what they respond to. You are working with people in large gatherings. Every time you speak, it is a sociological experiment, as you are watching the crowd's response and mass reactions, peer pressure and other phenomena.

Once I finally got to the Redwoods, and got out of my van, a silent wave came over me.

It was a very spiritual experience.

Walking through and seeing all those massive trees that were hundreds and hundreds of years old, it struck me how insignificant I truly was.

Now, I'm a very large man. I'm 6'11 and I tower over most people, and there I was standing in this Redwood Forest, staring up this tree I stood next to.

And I asked:

What are the things this tree has seen that it knows and understands more about the human mind, and the human condition that I could ever possibly begin to understand?

What are the pains that it knows? Maybe it knows the pains that I am suffering now, in this grieving cycle: the loss of my marriage and the loss of my family unit.

I began to weep.

I sat down next to that tree for several hours.

As the wave of emotion passed, I made mental notes of all the epiphanies of clarity and ideas that had come to my mind about the grieving cycle, about some of the baggage that I had taken into my own adult life from polygamy.

It was one of the most powerful experiences in my life.

As you heard me saying in my TEDx talk, *I choose clarity.* It was there in the Redwood Forests that the statement came to me.

I was leaning up against the tree when I whispered the words, *I choose clarity.*

After some time, I got back in my van and I drove over to the California coast to Fort Bragg.

I got out and I walked along the cliffs, seeing the vastness of the Pacific Ocean, once again realizing just how insignificant I actually was. And yet I was loved: I knew it in that moment, as I sat there on the cliffs of the Pacific Ocean.

The epiphany then came to begin recording myself. I pulled out my phone and made an audio recording. Granted, it was a very hard recording for me to hear with the wind in the background. But it was the first time I started recording my talk.

I had the prompting to begin doing this, as I watched out over the pacific.

For the rest of that trip, as I drove up the California coast, I made dozens of recordings and would listen to them dozens of times, back making notes each time, of things to change, add or redact.

Less is more, kept echoing in my head.

I made a dozen more recordings as I drove up to Brookings, Oregon, which was my last stop.

I stayed there for two days and just walked along the beach for hours, as I listened over and over again to the recordings, taking in the energy of the ocean and the purifying gusts of breeze.

On the last morning, I made one more recording. I didn't make one phone call this entire trip. I had gone on radio silence. I put my phone on airplane mode most of the time. I had vanished into the process.

It was now time to drive home.

I drove for fifteen straight hours, this time knowing my direction better. Fifteen hours straight and during that time, I just listened to my last production, my last draft, over and over again.

Seriously, I listened to it well over 50 times.

I was getting it embedded into my subconscious, beyond my short-term memory.

TEDxSaltLakeCity 2016, was two weeks away

Chapter 15
Don't Get Greedy

The week leading up to my TEDx Talk, I meet with several different fellow speakers, and also Jason and Beth one more time to go through my talk. As I sat with Jason and Beth, I had so many new things I wanted to share.

And this is normal, and also I started to do something that is too, quite normal:

Once you think you have your talk nailed down, you begin to think you can add in more.

"Oh well, I have time to throw in this idea, time to throw in that idea."

I started to get ambitious and greedy.

Also, I was getting bored!

I got so confident after my sabbatical/pilgrimage to California that I thought I could add in new things.

Thank goodness I did another trial run with Jason and Beth because I was trying to add in some new ideas off the cuff in that run; it was a train wreck.

Jason doesn't hold back, so luckily they were able to steer me back to the original plan and thread.

Less anecdotes, Lance!

Stay with what you know.

Be concise, be direct. You cannot be tangential on a TEDx talk. You have to stay focused. Again, you only have so many minutes and so many words to share... Make them count!

And then also I met with my peers and fellow speakers: Baya Voce, Kyl Meyers and Jamie Littlefield, different times throughout the week to practice my talk on them and they could practice on me.

It's hard to give a TEDx Talk to one person. Much more difficult than it is to speak to two thousand people in a room.

One person? That is very uncomfortable to do and I'm glad I did it.

There's great feedback to be had and you want your peers giving you their feedback, because if they have questions and they're smart people, think about all the questions the average Joe will have.

I had a weird challenge, in that throughout my first year as a motivational speaker, I had the constant feedback by fellow speakers and peers, *"Lance you're trying to speak to all the smart people and therefore you're losing all the regular people in the crowd. So, you have to dumb down your talks."*

Truly, that was the feedback.

Dumb down your talks.

I was speaking in too many abstracts, was what my speaker peers were telling me.

The biggest challenge Jason and Beth presented me with was to actually to start talking smart, in abstracts, and challenge people because the people who listen to TEDx Talks generally like to be challenged. And furthermore, they can handle being made to feel a little uncomfortable.

As I have said before, people remember things when they're slightly uncomfortable, just beyond their comfort zone.

With that being said, I was getting cocky. I thought I could just wing it and throw in cool ad-libs and tangents again... no good. And my peers reigned me back in.

Granted, part of it was because I was getting bored and this is normal, as well.

Again, I remind you: You are going to be tempted, right up to the very last minute to throw in some new ideas, because you don't want to waste this opportunity to share so many cool ideas.

But really you only have time for one to three ideas to share. Anything more than three ideas, people will forget them.

Remember this: three is a very powerful number. Teach people with three thoughts, three chains. Don't go for more than that. People remember things in threes. And especially within 18 minutes? You can't possibly expect them to remember more than three things.

So, leading up to your final week, get feedback from your coaches and do more practice rounds with your peers.

Resist the temptation to add on. As you grow in confidence with your talk, you are going to be tempted to throw more on it.

Don't.

Make it concise and direct. Stick with the plan.

Chapter 16
Title

Like it or not, title is very important. Clickbait works for a reason. Just like how people judge books by their cover, so too will they judge your TEDx talk before watching it. This will never change.

A perfect example of title influence occurred in December of 2016. Simon Sinek was a guest on the talk show, "Inside Quest." At first, the producers of that show uploaded a segment where he is speaking about millennial culture on their Facebook page, and titled it, "Simon Sinek on Millennials." It went a little viral to something like 200k hits.

But then something crazy happened. It was comical really. A small obscure firm called Delta Protective Services, re-uploaded that segment to their Facebook page, and titled it, "Millennials can be difficult to work with, here is why…" And then within 3 days, it amassed 50 million views.

First off, understand Facebook and YouTube are not friends. When you upload a raw file to your Facebook page, it does that cool thing where it automatically plays and has subtitles until you click on audio. That helps, but the most important thing was the title,

"Millennials can be difficult to work with… here's why."

Why did that work?

Because it was a title casting judgment. It was targeting and shaming a demographic, so that others could watch and be affirmed in their opinion, *"Yeah, those damn Millennials, so spoiled."*

Most people don't watch content to learn something new. This is a sad truth. Most watch content to have their opinions reaffirmed.

This is also why TEDx Talks don't necessarily go viral on Facebook, not only because the embedding of YouTube videos on Facebook is not as seamless as a raw upload, but also because you are watching a TEDx Talk to learn something new... and most people aren't interested in that. They are interested in being told that, *Yes, they already have all the answers.*

But if you have a good title for your TEDx Talk, it helps draw eyes and attention, even on Facebook viral trends.

With that Simon Sinek video suddenly going viral on a second round of retitle and rebranding, it is a confirmation that title is everything. And then the marketing. If your title can be confrontational or salacious, that is half the marketing battle right there.

You want to make sure that your title is something that's catchy, different but also appeals to human curiosity, not just scientifically for the smart people but for the regular people as well.

You want something that will appeal to everyone's baser curiosity. I had the luxury of talking about polygamy. Not only was I going for smart people who love TEDx Talks, I was going for all the people who have the stamina to endure reality TV shows like "Sister Wives." I was aiming for an eclectic audience, and that was my intention.

When I applied online back in the spring for TEDxSaltLakeCity, my title was "Polygamy and the Biology of Belief."

At first, I thought, *Oh, this is a smart sounding title for a TEDx Talk.*

It would have been a horrible title. Yet, the word polygamy is always going to be catchy, I knew that

Luckily, Jason Shepherd and my coaching staff, all sat me down one day and they asked, "Why don't you call it 'What is your polygamy?'"

I knew right away when they asked, that they were correct.

I was making a mistake in that I was overthinking things. I was thinking my title had to sound "smart." And also, I wanted to surprise people because I had such an interesting platform and I was going to flip it back on to everybody else, with the rhetorical question, "What is your polygamy?"

I didn't want to give away the "twist" too soon as though I was somehow directing an M. Knight Shyamalan movie.

I could see it very clearly then, my best strategy was to come out and challenge them immediately instead of waiting to do some plot twist towards the end or the middle of the talk.

No, I was far better off, getting right to the point, so everyone could see where I was going and enjoy the journey instead of wondering the entire time what my strategy was.

I realized it was far better for me to dump that question on them early and have them sit there in self-reflection and open to the parallels as I continued going on the journey.

If I waited too long, they would not have been making the effort to see how each stage of my talk applied to them.

But to come out right away and ask what is your polygamy, it makes them say, *"Yeah, what is mine?"*

There was going to be no confusion,
"What is your polygamy?"
For those in the crowd and those watching on their computers.

Let the crowd know immediately what they're getting into. When people click on your talk, they should know exactly what they're in for. I knew that was my best strategy.
"What is your polygamy?"
That is a grammatically incorrect question, someone will say, before clicking on my title.

The distorted syntax of the rhetorical question plus the keyword of polygamy, was a hook line of a title to get people curious.

I knew a lot of people were going to click on that because the word Polygamy is such a fascinating keyword, a hot topic, but also because of the format with which I posed it in, as a rhetorical question.

This came from the advice of my coaching staff and I'm very grateful for it. So, I'm going to challenge you.

Make sure your title, while still having some semblance of sounding smart, is very direct and has no plot twist.

Most importantly, don't take too long to get to the point of your talk.

I know when we're going to talk, we're very excited to "wow" people with our brilliance and our intelligence but don't forget there's going to be a lot of people in the crowd and online whose brains do not think as fast as yours. You have to be very careful, methodical and yes, you have to hold them by the hand sometimes and walk them through the journey and what they're in for.

I cannot possibly say that my way is the only way. My good friend, Baya Voce, who was the closing speaker that same year for TEDxSaltLakeCity 2016, has a very different experience.

She and I are on similar paths and excellent friends. We were the bookends for 2016, me the opener and Baya the closer and we were rooting for each other. Baya's process was very different from mine, however. This is not to say one was right and the other wrong.

Baya will honestly tell you, she didn't fully have her vision and thread of her talk until two weeks before her talk. She changed not only her script, but also her idea and pitch, several times throughout the process.

She had quite the journey. We spoke many times and I did my best to help her, but ultimately she had to choose what her talk was going to be for her, and then for everyone else who listened to it.

Your TEDx talk is your baby, and at the end of the day, the onus is on you.

Baya is a relationship expert and coach, and wanted to focus on "connection."

I was very proud of her when she closed the day with authority, especially knowing how pulled she was in different directions, with so many people giving their two cents to her through the process.

Then a quirky thing happened. I believe Baya gave the selection committee her title which was something about "Ritual and Connection." But then, the selection committee, while uploading the videos to the TEDx channel, chose a different title for her.

They called it, "The Simple Cure for Loneliness."

Something very interesting happened.

And I am completely fascinated with it.

Baya's talk really is not about curing loneliness; it's about the rituals of connection.

I'm not sure if the TEDx committee was planning on this, but the title "The Simple Cure for Loneliness" was a huge boon for Baya.

Loneliness is a very hot topic.

There are a lot of lonely people in the world today who no doubt are looking for answers. In this day and age of social media, people are lonelier than they've ever been.

I can only imagine how many people google the word, "lonely," and when they see *The simple cure for loneliness,* which is a very bold statement, you're setting yourself up for a lot of clicks and also a lot of disagreeing voices.

Yet, with my talk "What is Your Polygamy?" there was no real absolute opinion or challenging statement nor was it a voice of authority on something.

It was me just challenging everyone to look on their own selves. The title — "The Simple Cure for Loneliness" is making a very bold statement- *"I have the cure!"*

By nature, that's a controversial title.

It isn't salacious like polygamy, but just saying the *"simple cure for loneliness,"* is setting yourself up for a lot of scrutiny. Baya's talk has done very well, as of right now it has over

1,000,000 views. Yet, she's also gotten a lot of negative feedback from people disagreeing with her, finding the flaws in her talk because understandably, her talk does not really coincide with the title!

Baya knows this, as again she didn't select the title. Understandably, she was a bit frustrated when it all happened, but I smiled, laughed and I told her,

"Baya any views are good views. Any feedback is good feedback. Any press is good press. Eventually, you're going to get so much hate and criticism that you won't even care anymore. Welcome to the club."

Again, I can't say that my way is the only way because Baya and I had two very unique titles.

"The Simple Cure for Loneliness."
"What is Your Polygamy?"

Those are the kind of titles that people click on. Think about this - research it.

You want a title that makes people want to click on you.

Titles about relationships, again loneliness, sorrow, heartbreak, titles that pertain to human emotions, in my research, tend to gain far more clicks and views than those that do not.

I'm not saying you have to steer your talk to function solely on human emotions, but while TED stands for "Technology, Entertainment and Design," human emotion trumps everything. It trumps logic. It just does.

It Trumped the 2016 election. Puns intended.

You can spout facts, science and logic all you want but at the end of the day, humans will be ruled by their emotions, by what pulls at their heart strings, their basic human fascinations, loneliness, polygamy, religion, salacious things, which they can judge and be fascinated with.

People like to watch and judge things that make them feel something: Whether superiority or simple fascination.

There are so many clear titles that tap into this and thus explain why they do well, opposed to others.

Tony Robbins' TED Talk: "Why people do the things they do."

There is another TEDx talk out there, "How to be a Millionaire within 3 years."

Obviously, you can understand why that talk did well with over 3 million views. It isn't rocket science. Whether the content really was any good, the title alone, will get so many people who are obsessed with being wealthy, to click on it.

Take the time to research TEDx talks and what ones have over 1 Million views. Title has a lot to do with the success of your talk online. You could have the best presentation of the day at the live event, but if someone has a better title, chances are it will do better online.

This is just the way of the world.

You can pout about it, or play the game.

The title is the theme and it's establishing the thread and the arc throughout which your entire talk will carry and take the listeners on their journey.

Make sure it's a good title.

I cannot stress how important that is because again, people will always judge a book by its cover.

Chapter 17
Test Subjects

Practice makes perfect. I tell people all the time that as a basketball player, you can run sprints and condition all you want, but the best way to be in basketball shape is to play basketball.

Same thing with speaking. You can practice and rehearse by yourself and do this and that yada-yada. But the best way to be in speaking shape is to do a lot of speaking. Speak, speak and speak some more in front of people to become comfortable on the stage. Make it become like second nature to you. You want that stage to become your home.

Granted, a lot of you won't find paid speaking gigs but here's how you get opportunities to practice your TEDx Talk. Reach out to local Chambers of Commerce, Kiwanis Clubs, Rotary Clubs and Lions Clubs, etc.

Those types of organizations have a speaker or a presenter once a month. And because they don't normally pay- if they don't like your talk, they can't complain because, hey, you did it for free.

Reach out to those organizations in the months leading up to your TEDx talk. Even reach out to retirement homes and speak to older people. That'll be a great test, because if you keep those older folks engaged, and no one passes out on your time, or flat lines, you know are on the right track. Use those opportunities to gauge audience interest and interaction.

You can do Toastmasters; I did not. I had some friends that tried Toastmasters and they would go practice their talks and they get a lot of feedback and training on the body language. I have already addressed this and my opinion in regards to Toastmasters.

Find church or school opportunities, YMCA or any other groups, boy scouts even. Use those opportunities in the months and weeks leading up to your TEDx presentation to test and hone your craft in your message, but also your comfort level.

Once you know that you've been accepted to speak at TEDx, jump on this very quickly as a lot of times those events are booked months out before you get a chance to go talk to those clubs.

Use that opportunity to fine tune your message and continually go back to the drawing board. It is not important just for the development of your content, but more importantly to get comfortable on the stage.

If you want to be a great public speaker, do a lot of public speaking.

Closing note- Don't practice your talk on your closest friends and family. They are too close to see the forest through the trees, and most likely won't see where you are trying to go with the talk. Neutral listeners and strangers are the best for feedback during this stage.

Chapter 18
Slide Deck

If you watch my TEDx talk, all I used was four videos to carry the whole presentation. As a speaker, I make sure that I do not use bullet points. I don't know why people still continue to do this: they have presentations where they have bullet points laid out and all they do is simply read the bullet points. Anyone can read bullet points. You're wasting people's time and they will get bored.

If you must use a bullet point, don't read it verbatim. This is very boring for people and they will check out. When I speak to corporations or non-profits, I use videos and pictures. People remember images, because images and videos incite emotion- statistics and words not nearly as much.

You can throw all the statistics in the world at your audience, but if you don't have a video or picture attached to it, people are not going to remember it. Again, people remember what they feel, not what they hear.

I suggest strongly if you must use a statistic or bullet point, use very little and emphasize it with a video or picture to drive home an emotional connection.

Less is more.

You want your pictures and videos to carry you through the talk. My whole intention for use of my videos was to:

One, bring my audience into my world.

Two, carry me through as I memorized all of my crucial points around each slide and video. Each video was to incite a chain of thought that was to carry me through into the next video. They were tour guides not only for the audience but for me as well.

Those four videos became like four corners of my house, the frame of my talk.

They were the foundation and I knew each room that was every corner, and knew the flow of the house and what room led to the next. And I knew where exactly I was supposed to go from each room when I entered it, as my mind could begin to think ahead to the immediate next video/room, and not worrying about what was the video two slides ahead.

Most of my fellow TEDx speakers at Salt Lake did not use bullet points and I was proud of them.

Remember this when you are preparing your talk: if your bullet points are up there and you are simply reading your bullet points out loud, it becomes too much of a safety net.

It shows that you're not confident enough in your ability to narrate and carry people to an idea, but instead you have to have people read aloud with you. Too many speakers use this as a crutch

Even if you aren't reading the bullet points, too many bullet points and slides send the same message that you don't have the confidence, skill or persona to hold a room by yourself.

If you rely too heavily on your slides, it is brain numbing for the audience. It feels like a stuffy or lazy college lecture. As you prepare your images and slides, make sure they're fun and engaging. Make sure they incite emotion, challenge people and make them feel something.

Most importantly, don't use too much. Only use a few images.

I had a fellow speaker who always had an image of something in the background the whole time they talked. This was distracting.

I am now going to introduce you to the "Blank Black Screen."

Blank black screens are good. They are your friend.

I'm a big fan of the black screen. Meaning, between each video or image that I use, I have a blank black screen to click to instead of white or leaving the image up there.

Why?

Because when you go to black screen, the audience's attention will go back to you. And they can reconnect and engage with you. When people leave an image or a bullet point up for the entire time they're talking and then go to the next one, it keeps people distracted and will not allow them to fully connect or engage with you.

"Squirrel!"

You want people to connect with your content and story. But most importantly, you want people to connect with you.

If you don't like that idea, if you don't want all eyes on you, then why are you even on the stage in the first place doing public speaking? Why the hell are you even reading this book?

If you want to be a public speaker, you must learn to depend on your ability to stand there center stage and hold the audience's attention.

And when you do use images and videos, do not rely on too many. Less is more. Keep the audience enthralled. The blank black screen will leave them wondering what's going to be coming next. "What is behind the next door?"

Most importantly, it will also have them engaged and connected with you. That's what's going to carry the talk. You can have the most brilliant information in the world, the most well researched study and presentation, but if you are unable to engage and authentically stand in your space and connect with the audience, they will not remember the talk.

Whereas, you can have very boring, or ho-hum, mediocre or unoriginal content but if you're funny, engaging or just simply a speaker, then you will be just fine because that's what people will remember. Heart is more important than head.

Sad to say, this is the truth about public speaking.

Great content does not always necessarily translate into great viewership. Exciting presentations, engaged oration is what translates into viewership. More importantly, authenticity translates into viewership.

Excitement and joyful being in the moment, translates into viewership. It also just translates into simply being alive.

Chapter 19
Vocal Speed

Every speaker has their pace at which they speak. Some talk really fast and their diction remains intact. Some guys like Gary Vaynerchuck talk really fast and I can barely understand them. There is a time and place to switch the pace of your vocal speed. You don't want to speak at the same pace the entire talk. It is about peaks and valleys, same as in movies. Slow moments, building tension. Maybe some comedic relief and then fast climax.

I was cognizant of this as I practiced changing the pace through my talk and watched countless others who were successful.

There are times we must speak fast to create the urgency. There are times you speak very slowly, like when you are asking a rhetorical question, "What is your Polygamy?"

Let people absorb and think. If I had to ask what your polygamy is, and then go right to the next point, without giving people time to digest, the impact wouldn't have been as deep.

Give people enough time to process the information. Allow them to keep up with you especially when it is going into heavy content or scientific based research; you have to speak a little bit slower.

There are times when it's okay to pick up the pace, because you're getting excited and the content is lighter or getting funnier and then there are times we whisper.

Never underestimate the power of the whisper. Never.

Change the tone of your speech, the intonations; it keeps the audience engaged as compared to if you speak in a flat monotone the entire time. Again, I don't care how good your content is, people will get bored if you sound like a cardboard cutout.

I spent days walking around the neighborhood with my dog, talking to myself, people being worried that I was crazy. One time I was with my son, Simon, in the park and while he was on the swings, I was talking to myself and a lady came and took her child away; her child was standing too close to me. She gave me a look because she truly thought I was crazy.

And I didn't care- because I kind of was crazy at that point. I had lost my mind. It was two days before TEDxSaltLakeCity and my mind was in a state of automation.

I practiced not only on changing the tone of my voice, but also the volume.

A very important thing too, is that you do not want to speak from your throat. Rather, speak from your ribs.

DO NOT speak from your throat.

People who speak from the throat, are too soft spoken. It is difficult to hear people when they speak from the throat and also one of the first things of human nature when we get nervous or emotional is for our throat to clamp up.

It is natural instinct for us to clamp our throat when we foresee pain.

It's a defense mechanism so that if you get hit or punched, you will be able to retain some of the oxygen in your lungs.

You have to learn to practice speaking from your ribs and your belly.

I like to do the image work that when I'm speaking, the air and the words are actually in my rib cage and not just my lungs. The air is all over my chest and torso.

That's where the words are at and I don't have to pull the words from my head or throat or from my mouth. Rather, they're actually in my rib cage and I can see those words and I am able to push them out with great force. The words course in the blood, through the muscles of my ribs and heart space.

I know some people think image work is ridiculous. But so is being cynical.

That's fine, but I use a lot of image work. I always pretend or envision that the words are in my chest and so when I speak,

I have to speak from my ribs to push the words up, with the power of my ribs and lungs, not through my throat.

Whenever I have spoken through my throat, when I get choked up, I lose my voice, because again, the throat is constricting.

You'll see a moment happening in "What is Your Polygamy?" when I was speaking on the stage and I began recalling the memories of my marriage.

I had a moment there that I began to lose it, and I had a choice to try to speak through it, to speak through the pain that was in my body at that time with the images and memories that were coming to me.

But instead, I chose to simply take a little step back and take a deep breath.

Deep breath. And gathered it in my ribs and lungs.

After a few counts, I resumed and began speaking from my ribs and my chest. You'll notice the change in power, and emphasizing through my ribs and for the rest of the talk, I spoke with power and I spoke with authority through heavy, heavy content.

I began to have the images of the words coming up through my belly, through my ribs through my lungs and I kept breathing deep into my ribs pushing from there. Not from my throat.

If you find yourself ever getting emotional on stage, stop and take a deep breath. Don't try to squeal through it.

Just stop and take a breath.

When you try to speak through the emotion, your voice can get to a high pitch and you start to break down and that makes everyone uncomfortable. It is just an awkward moment.

I saw this so much as a kid in church growing up. People sharing their testimonies, and once they get emotional, they try to squeak through it at a high pitch.

Just uncomfortable.

For everyone.

Sorry.

Whereas, being able to channel your emotions, not suppressing them, has a far greater impact.

You can even say to the crowd, *"I'm getting a little bit emotional. I'm sorry. I need to take a breath."*

This is fully okay to do, and in fact is a sign of emotional health and maturity.

The crowd will fully engage with you and they will empathize with you and acknowledge that you were willing to be vulnerable and publicly acknowledge the difficulty. And they will allow you the moment.

It's okay to take a breath and gather yourself. Breathe through your lungs, through your chest and come back with more authority than ever before.

You will be able to make a very memorable talk, if you do this. That's what people will remember. Not so much the content, but how you powered through heavy content. But that will actually amplify your content.

Controlling your emotions, while allowing the audience to connect with you is a huge boon for you. Remember, take a breath, speak slowly, speak deep, speak with authority.

Maybe you are worried about time and so are speaking quickly through your throat. If it's a contest between time and composure, always err on composure.

If you're worried about that eighteen-minute mark and are cramming through a lot of emotion speaking with a high voice unable to control your emotions, it will be a double disaster, and two negatives don't make a positive. And you always need to account for your talk to be at least one minute longer than planned.

* Again, plan for at least one more minute of length when you are finally on the stage, as opposed to when you practice it.

Speak slowly, speak under control, and speak through your belly, through your ribs, into your lungs. Always speak with composure.

Don't suppress your emotions; allow people to feel it and connect with it, as you want to keep your emotions always there, but just beneath the surface, just boiling. But, don't ever let them overspill.

Allow the audience to connect with you and those emotions and then allow the audience to feel safe knowing you have control over your emotions.

The last thing the audience wants is to be responsible for your emotional health and well being when they have their own to worry about.

Chapter 20
Wardrobe

Are we really going to talk about something so vain and trivial like what you are going to wear?

Yes. Yes, we are.

A month before TEDxSaltLakeCity was slated to begin on September 17, 2016, the selection committee informed me that I would be the opening speaker.

No pressure.

No pressure at all!
9:00 AM on a Saturday morning.
I am not a morning person, FYI.

I still chuckle when I think about it. It's very hard to get people riled up at 9:00 AM, especially on a Saturday morning.
I knew I had my work cut out for me, but I knew I could do it. Heck, as the center position of my basketball teams, it was my job to start the opening tip-off, so I knew I could do this.

If I was going to be an opening speaker, I better come out looking ready to get the show started. I had to do this with a bang.

I had done enough events by now to know that the opening speaker is very, very important in setting the tone for the rest of the event. Whether it's a corporate event or a TEDx event, doesn't matter.

I needed to come out and get people ready: ready to do this thing for the rest of the day. Get them inspired, get them emotionally invested, get them motivated. You know, "Beast Mode."

Not only did I have to share my story of "What is your Polygamy" and share an idea worth spreading, I also had to get people pumped up to endure the seven-hour day.

And I'm glad the TEDx committee entrusted me to do that. But also, I knew since I was going first, I would be the first one to get it out of the way and enjoy the rest of the day. Unlike my poor friend Baya Voce, who was the closing speaker, and had to fidget and squirm for seven hours. She was bouncing off the walls by the time it was her turn.

I knew that if I was going to start the day out with a bang, I had better make sure that I was looking sharp.

I went through dozens of ideas about wardrobe.
I'm not the flashiest dresser, mind you. I don't "peacock."
If I could go stand on a stage and speak in my basketball sweats, I would. But, if I'm going to be up there talking about leadership, I better look the part of a leader or at least try to.

Now, on the flipside, no one likes that guy in a sport coat and slacks with his penny loafers, who looks like he's a member of the yacht club. Nobody likes that guy, seriously.
I promise.
Everyone is going to be waiting for your "pitch" if you dress like that.

Yeah, I know you are trying to look like you're a leader and a specialist in the field in what you're going to talk about.
But the majority of people sitting in a crowd, they're business casual.

If you come across as too well dressed you're going to come across as too stuffy. And people will immediately be on their guard.

Be careful with how you think about dressing.
I was very proud of my fellow speakers at TEDxSaltLakeCity. Some guys wore sport coats. But they did it tastefully with jeans or other clothes and they didn't look too pretentious.
I flirted with the idea of a sport coat, but I knew I was never going to wear a tie. That was way too formal if you watch TEDx events. TEDx Talks are usually dressed very business casual and every now and then, you'll see someone talking in a tie and suit, and again, my instinct is to distrust them. It just is.

Maybe all this stems from my childhood in the 80's when my parents were big into Amway- shady MLM types in their fancy suits.

As a public speaker myself, if I'm telling you that I distrust people when they're too well dressed on stage, what does that say about what the ordinary person in the crowd is thinking? The ordinary 9-to-5 worker who is tired of dealing with the "man" all the week and wants to come to your TEDx event and be inspired and hear interesting ideas?
They probably don't want to see someone who is too well dressed, too fancy, that looks like the person they hand in quarterly reports to.

Granted, you don't want to walk out in a dumpy T-shirt with wrinkles and holes in your jeans. You want to look respectable. You want to be sexy. Sexy is good.
Basketball players have a universal motto.
"Look good, you feel good. You feel good, you play good." Poor syntax but you get the gist.
You want to look like you can walk into a Christmas dinner with your family, sans ugly sweater, or maybe you do, I

don't know, you could probably get away with that if you had the right amount of confidence. You just want to dress with swagger.

Again, I had the idea of maybe wearing a sport coat and I was getting a couple of reclaimed, vintage sport coats tailored to fit my size as I had lost a lot of weight since I retired from basketball, but luckily I'm glad my tailor is such a perfectionist that he didn't have any of my new sport coats ready, and so I had to go with a very casual, confident sporty look.

Thank goodness my very close friend Brian Savage and his husband had recently moved to town from Chicago and offered to help me shop for clothes:
Queer Eye for the Straight Guy at my side.

Bryan was able to give me very valuable feedback on a lot of things that just were not going to work. Namely a sport coat that I thought I might try to pull off against a pair of gray jeans that would clash, unbeknownst to my palate.
I knew I wanted *black*. I just knew I wanted black. I don't know what it was about the black that was calling my name, but I knew I wanted to wear black.

But also, I knew I wanted to highlight it with red as my last name is Allred. But also those were the colors of TEDx. I had watched a lot of talks where people's colors have dramatically clashed with their surroundings and the red TED logo and it was actually distracting.
The TED logo is very red, even more red in person, I promise you, and you're going to have dark spots in the background and the lighting will be right on you, highlighting all your pores, even your past sins.
Don't clash.
Blend.

Now granted, we can't all start wearing black and red now. This isn't a prep school. TEDx Talks are not supposed to be uniform. But you can do a little bit to make sure you blend in well, because you don't want to "*Peacock.*" You don't want your wardrobe distracting people from what you're talking about.

You want to be dressed well enough that you look classy and you look confident. And then once people think you're confident, they then will believe you are trustworthy and will start connecting with you on a deeper level.

Your physical appearance plays a big role in whether people believe you are credible. You want people to trust you and go deeper with you, to where they don't even notice your physical appearance anymore.

Your physical appearance and wardrobe is simply a door that people will choose to enter or not, deciding if they want to hear more of what you have to say.

The day before TEDxSaltLakeCity, Brian and I did some last minute miracle shopping. I was a bit stressed and still hadn't found *THE* outfit. I had a nice pair of black jeans, which were perfect. And I knew I wanted to wear something that would go with the black jeans. I had a crush on the jeans and the black and white Puma shoes.

But the day before, with no shirt? With my size?

Do you know how frustrating it is to shop for clothes when you are 6'11?

People say they wish they could be tall, but they have no idea the frustration of clothes shopping and door frame colliding with your skull. It's damn near discriminatory.

Luckily, at a last stop, we went to Dillard's; it has a big and tall section. But my skepticism was high as most "Big and Tall" places skew to fat people. It is unfair.

Brian and I looked through a lot of shirts- *fun shirts this, cute shirts that, which would kind of go with the black jeans... kind of.*

Maybe some amoeba patterns? That would be trendy!

And then a beam of light appeared from the heavens, with a chorus of cherubim serenading its glow upon a rack of shirts. Brian found this black shirt that wasn't too black and it perfectly complimented my jeans, as it was just a different off color black.

As soon as I put it on, we both knew it was the perfect shirt.

Thank you, rose-cheeked baby angels.

However, Brian and I disagreed on a major issue shortly after, in that Brian said,

"Okay, you don't really want to wear anything underneath it. If you do you, you want to have it to be a V-neck and you want it to be a very soft color."

I took Brian's advice at first, frowning that I would not be getting the "Red" that I wanted when I went home that night. Because, what do I know about fashion, right?

That night, as I paced back and forth in the dark, rehearsing like I was on opiates, I had a sudden burst of defiance.

You know what? No! I'm going to wear a very bright red underneath the black. I am going to peacock! I will peacock and I will like it!

Needless to say, once I stepped off the stage following my performance, Brian and his husband, both of whom were braggers about their fashion degrees and savvy, congratulated me on my choice, acknowledging that I went with the right call with my red shirt.

Normally, people make fun of how bland my clothing and fashion is, especially my brother who throws out his wardrobe with the seasons.

So, for me, it's not every day I get praise from "fashion experts." And so, when I get the compliments, I take them.

Chapter 21
Brain Cramp

The night before my TEDx talk, I paced back and forth for hours, reciting and reciting.

Don't be alarmed if you lose your mind along the way, somewhere between the 178th recital of your talk, and when you finally start to notice people distancing themselves from you at the park.

Something funny is going to happen to your brain when you start preparing for your TEDx Talk:

You'll be surprised at how much of your brain's data power and storage is taken over by your TEDx talk. It is completely normal.

I truly, physically felt like half of my brain was completely dedicated to the TEDx Talk. It was consuming everything, all the blood sugar.

I had no time, nor cognitive reasoning to be a good dad. I had no time to feed myself. I had no time to take a nice proper shower. I always had to be talking, rehearsing.

My three-year-old son, Simon, had to ask me on several occasions, "Dad, please stop talking to yourself. Please, Dad? Pleaaaaaase?"

Such was my state as I kept walking around the house and mumbling to myself like a crazy person. I would take my dog on a walk mumbling to myself like a madman talking to his long lost friends who died in Vietnam. I got plenty of crazy looks from people. Plenty of them. And frankly, I didn't even have the brain space to care.

I knew this TEDx Talk was an important play for what I was trying to do for my ultimate goal through all the speaking, which is to speak to as many schools and kids as I possibly can.

Speaking to corporations and non-profits is fun, yes, but my whole goal is to speak to kids. Teenagers that "get it," are my favorite audience; their brains are really coming to their own, learning and how to question authority and reality. Teaching teenagers how to be leaders of their own lives is what it is all about.

I knew this TEDx Talk was a huge opportunity for me to potentially reach millions of people, and also have a beautifully finished product (a complete talk) in 10 to 15 minutes.

The pressure was on and I just didn't care if people thought I was crazy. Whenever I took a shower, I was talking to myself. Every time I drove around town, I was just talking to myself. I didn't listen to music anymore. Nope, I was just talking to myself. Rehearsing and reciting.

I was just talking to myself memorizing it so much so, that it became deeply embedded into my subconscious. There is a very fine line of people who know their talks and those who are simply "reading" to you, such is its place in their short-term memory.

You don't want to be that person. You don't want to read. When your talk is simply stored in your short-term memory that is "reading."

I chose to remember my talk so well that it became embedded, deeply embedded into my subconscious that I didn't even have to think about it anymore.

And if I didn't have to think, then I could then go back to being in the moment and let my body language tell the story, let my emotions tell the story, where the words were just coming out and my body's job was to truly convey and connect the story.

I could simply just let my body move with where the words were going. I did not practice or rehearse the body language. I truly didn't. I knew that they would come out in the moment on the stage.

I did have one piece of coaching as far as body language that I did receive and utilize, and that was if when you're telling a dialogue, you switch sides to face different people while talking. That's it. Other than that, I never really truly practiced my body language.

I told myself when I get on the stage that I was just going to feel all the words and allow them to come out. And my body will do what it needs to do.

Maybe that was from years of being a basketball player and a world of experience of performing in front of people that naturally, physically performing just came to me, as there was no scripted behaviors or patterns in basketball in the moment. It was all improvisation as a basketball player.

It shouldn't be a surprise to tell you, how bored and sick I became of my talk.

I had rehearsed, and practiced, and scripted my talks, so many times that it truly was stuck so deep in my subconscious, that I began to get sick of it.

But I knew I couldn't let off.

That's when you know you're on the right path. When you are just so "over it."

But what really surprised me, was what happened the night before my talk-

I started to forget lines.

That let me know that my brain was tired.

It also told me that I was ready and my brain was bored. I had done my job.

When you start to forget lines that you remember so well, it means you've done enough.

And I knew when I was forgetting my lines that my brain was ready to shut down and charge for the next day, just as my brain and body did before basketball games.

In my basketball days, whenever I showed up to an arena was when I was most tired. Two hours before a tip-off, I just wanted to take a nap every time. I wanted to sleep. It wasn't because I was lazy or unmotivated. It was my body shutting down, storing its energy and preparing to perform, to exert tremendous amounts of energy.

When I started forgetting my lines, I wasn't panicked. It let me know that I was ready and something big was coming.

It was time to go to sleep and charge for the day.

Don't get discouraged if you start forgetting lines when you feel like you've had them all memorized. It means you are ready for the moment.

Chapter 22
Never Assume

Never assume that you have all the answers and that you have everything memorized and more importantly, never assume you have the dates and times correct.

I was the opening speaker for TEDxSaltLakeCity and the rehearsal day the day before, Friday morning, we were to begin speaking at 10:00 AM. We were going to do a dry run through everyone's talks. This is the first time that my speaker coaches were going to hear my final draft.

I felt I had it done. I had it ready to go and I did, but here's the one mistake and one assumption I made and I'm very glad that I did not think that I had all the answers- Because the rehearsal began Friday morning at 10:00 AM, I had it in my mind to be prepared to speak Saturday morning at 10:00 AM.

Luckily enough, my parents asked what time they should be there at TEDxSaltLakeCity and I told them to arrive at 9:45, to get a good seat.

My mom checked back and asked, "Lance are you sure? Because I believe the schedule says it begins at 9."

I checked myself and then I called up my friend Baya and I asked, "What time are we supposed to meet there as a team before it begins? "

Baya laughed and responded, "Lance, we meet at 8 am. The show starts at 9:00."

Thank goodness for my parents.

Being the opening speaker, it would have been a disaster. If I hadn't had asked, I would have shown up at 9 am, just as the show began.

Don't be like me and assume. Double-check and then check again. Check everything multiple times. Contact people and confirm. Confirm with the fellow speakers regarding everything about the schedule.

I know this sounds mundane and trivial but in my case had I not, it would have been a disaster

Chapter 23
Know Your "Why"

Yes, my son, Simon, is my greatest inspiration. He is the impetus behind everything that I do and I knew this TEDx Talk was going to help me professionally, so I could better provide for him as a father.

Furthermore, I also knew that I was helping others by educating them about polygamy.

But there also was another why.

Two different things;

I have a very close family friend and mentor, Christy Foster, who also grew up in polygamy with me. She is a cranial-sacral specialist, has a brilliant mind and is always so insightful. She was able to impart me with great wisdom when I saw her the day before TEDxSaltLakeCity. She and I were able to go over some things and then she was able to inspire me with the thought:

"Lance, you aren't selling or taking anything, all you are doing is giving them a gift."

Another mentor, who is also a professional speaker, Tiffany Peterson, shared a similar message with me the night before, "Go and love them."

That morning, I woke with a start at 5 am, ready to go and seize the day. I got dressed, putting on my fancy new clothes, had my haircut done the night before, looking all sharp but not too sharp like I had spent two hours in front of the mirror, but preferably just ten minutes.

I arrived at TEDxSaltLakeCity, at 7 am still on high alert that I might miss something due to the near miscommunication about when it actually started, so I wasn't going to leave anything to chance.

I went to the green room or speakers room in the back of the building and laid down on the ground for about 30 minutes, just breathing, doing my breathing exercises, 10-10-10: 10-second count breathing in, 10-second count holding it in, and 10- second count letting it out.

All the while, focusing, imaging, forecasting. Imagery is very powerful, not just the imagery of what the breath does when it enters your body but I was imagining me in the future, an hour from then, on the stage, how I was going to respond to each word.

I was so confident that I had the entire talk deeply embedded into my subconscious that I could now just focus on what my body would be doing and how I would be dancing with the stage.

It was then that someone came and kicked my foot and asked me if I was okay. They thought maybe I had passed out or hyperventilated as I sat up, and smiled, and said, "No, I'm fine, I'm just doing my breathing exercises."

At that point, all the other fellow speakers began to file in, and we had to have a team meeting at 8 am to group photos and wish each other the last, *good lucks,* as we all began to split up and go to our seats.

The first three speakers: me, Kyl Meyers and Dave Durocher, went downstairs into the green room, pacing back and forth, preparing ourselves.

Little by little, the minutes crept up, seeming to take an eternity to pass.

I was ready to scream at people to stop approaching me, my full diva mask on, because I was just ready to go on the stage and get it done.

I'm the type of person that if I found a cliff above deep water or about to go skydiving off an airplane, I don't ever go look over the cliff. I don't stand there looking deep into the abyss.

I don't.

I just say, *"Okay, it's time to do it,"* and then I just run and take off.

Spending your time staring down the throat of fear doesn't help you.

And so I did my best to just stay in the moment, imagining each word, each moment with each word, so that when my time came, when my name was called I was ready to get on the stage and just do it. Get it out of the way.

The minutes passed by slowly. I got my cup of coffee and I continued to pace back and forth and the show began.

The Emcee went out there onto the stage and she began to introduce all the sponsors and the vision at TEDx and TEDx Talks and why they are and what their mission and purpose is.

This was the worst part.

It was 9 am, but I actually wouldn't be on stage until 9:20. That was when I laid down in the corner of the backstage and began doing breathing exercises again. Thus, several more people thought I had passed out and everyone came and checked on me, doing their best to interrupt my flow.

Diva mode, people!

Those last 20 minutes, felt like 200.

The process of watching her introduce the sponsors and go through the video intros, was dentistry work.

I was pacing back and forth, back and forth, ready to do this thing, but then a moment of fear, immense fear, came over me.

What if I stutter or what if I fail and what if I get my words and in that moment, I lose clarity?

I had broken my rule and I was now looking over the edge of the cliff.

But then I had an epiphany, a remembrance come to me and it was this:

I am not selling anything. I'm not taking anything. I am merely giving them a gift, all the people who are out in the seats.
I am giving them a gift.

I choose to love them. I choose to give them my love. I choose to be vulnerable. I choose to be authentic. I am not selling anything nor am I taking anything. I am merely giving them a gift.

And then after that last thought, immense power came to my body when I said,

Mother Earth,
Thank you for everything: for all of my experiences, for the painful memories and the happy memories and all the memories in between.
I am a child of you. I am a child of the earth. It is the earth and that source from which I have come and it is the earth that has carried me through my travels around the world giving me those experiences.

What a gift the earth had given me with all these experiences. And so it was my gift, in turn, to take these experiences and apply them and allow millions of others to learn from them, to help them gain clarity.

"Mother Earth, this is my gift to you," were my last words. And then my name was called.

When you are in a space of giving, and not selling anything nor taking anything, but in a space of giving, you cannot fail.

This, I promise you: you cannot fail.

Chapter 24
The Zone

As I stepped onto that TEDx stage and stared at the thousands of people looking at me, I had full clarity.

I knew then in that moment that is where I was supposed to be. Nowhere else.

All of my hundreds of hours of preparation for TEDxSaltLakeCity alone had prepared me for this, not to mention all of my thousands of hours on my book tour across the country, speaking to kids in basketball settings, and also the thousands of hours as a basketball player and performer, preparing for the stage, preparing for the public eye of scrutiny and criticism.

I had developed a very thick skin and I was ready for this, not to mention all the experiences of my childhood, growing up in polygamy, and the subconscious patterns that had plagued me for so long, which I was now exorcizing, baptizing on that stage, and potentially in front of millions.

That moment then and there, was arguably the most clarity I've ever had in my entire life and that's saying a lot because I have had many profound moments, especially when my son was born.

At that moment I was so present: there was no past, there was no future.

It was only about that moment and I saw my words begin to appear before me, like the Star Wars opening credits, spanning up and out, over the crowd.

I could see all of my words perfectly timed, in rhythm and I knew exactly where they were, and I didn't have to focus on them.

The words were already there. They were going to come, all I had to do was feel them; feel that moment, feel those emotions, feel the emotions that the words were the catalyst for. To allow those words to carry the emotions.

It was simply my job at that point to be present, to be a conduit, to be a vessel and guide into a perspective and experience for others to join if they chose, with the Head, Heart and Soul.

That's all my job was. My job wasn't to try to convince or win anybody over or have people suddenly like me or get the standing ovation.

My job was to simply be a messenger in that moment, which is what I had promised Mother Earth. It was my gift to her and she would do with it whatever she wanted. Whether the people liked it or whether they didn't, it was not my responsibility anymore.

I had surrendered the burden of responsibility. I had allowed it to be what it would choose to be. It was no longer my burden to give the perfect TEDx talk.

It was my job to simply be in the moment and be a messenger. And I stayed in that moment and I allowed myself to feel. I allowed myself to face the many emotions that I never did as a boy growing up in polygamy. I allowed myself to grieve.

I allowed myself to go through all of those emotions: denial, anger, bargaining and acceptance.

In 13 minutes, I went through them all. I felt all of them. And then I allowed myself to feel gratitude.

I baptized myself on the stage in front of thousands and now millions of people.

I allowed myself to be human.

I allowed myself to be flawed.

I allowed myself to not be perfect, to just be me-

Lance, a child of the Earth, who for that brief moment was simply, Lance.

I saw the memories of my childhood, the good and the bad. Of loved ones now gone and my parents and siblings now still alive with all the memories made together, and the impact they have had on my life.

I saw my basketball coaches, the good and the bad, the traitors and the tyrants, and the friends. And the mentors and my teammates that I have loved along the way.

I saw my son. And with that, I saw his mother, my ex-wife, my love. A great love that would not be coming back. And the many memories that were not coming back.

I allowed those memories to remain there in their rightful place- in the past. And I allowed myself to grieve it.

In that moment when the memories of the pain became so great, I was forced to take a step back. And for five seconds, I just grieved. And I allowed myself to grieve.

I allowed all those memories to come through me. And I felt them.

And then chose to accept it, and find gratitude in them and my current place.

And to accept the unknown future of what lay ahead. And release it.

Then I chose clarity. I chose the clarity that life has not looked like what I expected it to look like. But it has been a great journey and therefore a great reward. And I was able to breathe in those emotions. And then for the remainder of my talk I chose to speak with authority, speak with clarity, speak with authenticity.

I knew my place in that moment. I knew who I was: I was Lance. Not Lance, the basketball player. Not Lance, the speaker. I was Lance, the child of this earth, nothing more nothing less.

That was a moment of pure peace and clarity. I knew I was loved unconditionally.

As I closed, I saw the images of me as a little boy. Working so hard, practicing for hours in speech therapy, trying to learn how to say his "r's"; how to read people's lips and read words out of books and watch people say those words, and figure out the syntax and the tone shifts of the vowels and taking the context of a conversation and responding in kind.
The image of that boy who worked so hard, who just so badly wanted to be "normal," who wanted to be heard, who wanted to communicate.

I allowed that boy in that moment to come on the stage with me.

Some may call me crazy but I would believe in quantum physics. If an electron can be in two places at one time- why then could five-year-old me not come with me onto that stage in that moment where I could allow him to see the many great and wonderful things he was going to do?

I allowed my five-year-old self to be with me on that stage, to be my partner as we stood in our authentic space as I said goodbye and I thanked them and took a step back and bowed.
And then the standing ovation.

Not because of the well-timed videos or the hundreds of hours I practiced my speech nor the perfectly placed words, nor the very effective thirteen hundred words that I had to make count with every single breath.

While all those helped, the reason why I got the standing ovation, was because I chose authenticity. I chose to be vulnerable. I chose clarity.

Chapter 25
Exit Stage

You don't want to stand on the stage for too long, neither do you want to just simply rush off the stage when you are done. You have given the audience a gift, allow them to give you a gift in turn and applaud you.

There's timing to it. Again, don't leave too soon. Allow the audience to give you their ovation and then don't stay too long because that gets awkward.

I chose to stay there for eight seconds, then I exited the stage.

As I walked off the stage, I was able to detach from the crowd and barely make it off the stage before I kneeled over, crying.

Jason Shepherd was there watching me the whole time from the side curtain and he met me and gave me a hug. Then Kyl Meyers and Davis Smith, my fellow speakers. I sobbed. I was overtaken with so much emotion.

Sure, it was a combination of stress and pent up energy, which I had been siphoning for weeks on end now, but also it was me coming through that grief cycle and all the emotions that I allowed to come to the surface, but had not allowed myself to feel, until then.

When you step off the stage, do not be overwhelmed or surprised if you have the sudden urge to break down and cry. It's a near blinding intense moment.

This is one of my benchmarks as a speaker that lets me know whether I did a good job not just at TEDxSaltLakeCity, but at any public event: If I can bow out and leave the stage, and I have that wave of emotions come over me, it lets me know that my emotions were there and I was authentic and the crowd felt something.

It's completely normal to have this rush of emotions come over you when you exit the stage. Don't judge yourself. Don't be embarrassed about it.

As I got done hugging everybody, I quickly snuck downstairs to the green room where I was by myself.

I sat down and I sobbed. I just sobbed. For about five minutes, I just cried.

I was so relieved that it was over and I was also so grateful for the opportunity that I was given. And furthermore, I was proud. I was proud of the hard work that I had put in; the hard work five-year old me had put in.

And I was proud of my son, Simon, for how much of a teammate he was for me and how he inspired me in his three years of age. He is always rooting for me as he could tell when I was doing something important and allowed me to walk around the house talking to myself. And he was always so supportive of me, and waited patiently until I was done and then asked if we could play dinosaurs.

I was so proud to be his dad. I always will be.

We make a good team, my Simon and I. And I was proud that I did not let him down.

And there's nothing to be ashamed about, being proud of your yourself, especially raised in Mormon culture where we're taught that no one likes a braggart and so you are always supposed to be self-effacing. Therefore, to this day, I have a hard time taking compliments.

But in that moment, for the rest of the day, I allowed myself to take a compliment, and be proud of what I had achieved and what had been done.

And I also know that fifty percent of it was hard work and the other fifty percent was the inspiration that came from other places, Source or Mother Earth.

Inspiration comes from many places and again I knew I was only a messenger. I was simply a vessel. Never forget this truth.

Allow yourself to feel those emotions when you step off the stage. It's completely normal. It means you're human and most likely also means you did a wonderful job, connecting with other humans- to feel the human experience.

Chapter 26
Shaking Hands, Kissing Babies

Being the opening speaker, once I was done, for the rest of the day I had to make myself available for V.I.P. room lunches, sit-downs with sponsors and other things. This was tough because I was exhausted.

I had exerted so much energy on the stage that I was ready to go home and take a nap but I also still had an adrenaline high; it was a weird dichotomy. One minute, I wanted to sleep, the next, I was ready to say *"Hi,"* to everyone like the Energizer Bunny.

Be emotionally prepared for this when you speak at your TEDx event, or any event really. You're going to have to shake hands and kiss babies. It's part of the deal.

Even if you're an introvert and you don't like socializing, if you want to be on the TEDx stage, make sure you powder up your social skills a bit, because you're going to have people that you've never met before and might never see again, coming up to talk to you about all sorts of things, professional and personal.

This is what happens when you're a public speaker: people connect with you. They feel as if they know you and they feel safe with you, which by the way, is what you were asking for and so you have to be ready to own that.

You're even going to have a lot of people come up to you and tell you their stories. And in a way, you have become the armchair psychiatrist.

When they see you on the stage exerting so much authenticity, they feel the need to do the same as well. People will come up to you, shake your hand, hold you in one place for a long time and feel the need to tell you their story.

Be prepared for this, it's part of the job detail. I listened to dozens of people tell me their personal stories throughout the rest of the day and it only made me more tired but again, it's part of what I signed up for.

Balance it out by sneaking out when you can and going to a quiet room and just lay down on your back, butt up against the wall, with your feet elevated 90 degrees. It is my favorite way of winding down.

And then once the event concludes, you will go to a mixer. Maybe, maybe not, but we did at TEDxSaltLakeCity. You will be so tired, but you will also want to go, because this will be the last time you see all of your new friends together again.

And then you will say goodbye. And things will go back to "normal." Back to your normal, everyday life.

And it will suddenly be over. And it will seem so quiet when you get home.

Hauntingly quiet.

Even your brain is so quiet.

And you may even feel alone. Too alone.

Chapter 27
Post-Wedding Blues

Having played in the NBA, I was well prepared for and expecting the brutal comedown of the "high."

I knew that with the blinding high, like I experienced of being called up to the NBA and also having that happen with my marriage, the blinding high of your wedding and then the next day sadness, is something called, "The post-wedding blues. "

This is actually very common. And brutal. And that is normal too.

Depression runs in my family and I am someone throughout my life that has struggled with depression and anxiety, even suicidal depression. Genetically, my family is predisposed to have serotonin imbalances. Serotonin is what allows your brain to process and filter thoughts and move onto the next thought.

But when you have an imbalance or shortage of serotonin, that's when obsessive thoughts tend to stay. You cannot push them out. Serotonin is kind of like Draino for your brain, is the best analogy I can give you.

It helps you unclog your brain and get new thoughts in.

Leading up to TEDx, I was prepared for this: a serotonin shift, because I have learned that not only majorly negative events but also milestones and/or major happy events can trigger a serotonin imbalance, even depression. Hence, the common phenomenon,"Post-Wedding Blues."

Expecting this, the week leading up to my TEDx talk, I began taking what is called the natural supplement, 5-HTP, which helps organically balance your serotonin levels.

I didn't think to warn my TEDxSaltLakeCity speakers about this until after a couple days following the event, because I woke with a deep silent loss.

My son was with his mom that weekend and I woke up and I was by myself and my brain was incredibly confused.

It didn't know what to do with itself because over half of my brain's energy and power have been filtered and dedicated to the TEDx talk but now that it was over, I felt like I had this empty side of my brain that just didn't know what to do with itself.

It felt hollow. Literally, it felt hollow.

For the remainder of that day as I was walking around, I was still reciting parts of the talk to myself, such was the habit.

To cope, I began to clean my house, like a deep bleach clean, and trust me, it was the only thing I felt like doing. I did not want to socialize.

When you speak on the stage, you are exerting so much energy, so much emotional energy and you are taking everyone else's energy back onto you, whether you like it or not. It is draining and you need to detach and recharge. I like to clean and do laundry when I get to that point.

I disappeared for two days. I didn't talk to anybody. I didn't turn on the phone. I just checked out. I just deep cleaned the house and listened to music: that's all I did. It is a perfectly normal emotion, to want to detach and become a hermit.

Such was my state of myopic solitude, that I failed to think what my friends were going through until Baya called me and asked me if I could meet her for coffee the next day and I was glad to do so.

It was quite funny actually because Baya is a relationship coach and yet Baya had never heard about "post-wedding blues."

She was a wreck.

She was all over the place, coming down off that huge high. She had given so much of her life preparing for her talk, it consumed her like it consumed me and everyone else and she thought she was going crazy. She thought she was depressed, she thought she was sad.

She was all those things.

Baya is a very positive and upbeat person who coaches people to get out of their ruts, and yet here she was, in a rut.

But I understood what it was. It wasn't sadness or depression.

She was having the "post-wedding blues" and it was completely normal, and I was glad that I was able to be there for her in that moment, to let her know that it was a common feeling and experience and that she start taking 5-HTP.

This made me realize I should call my friends and fellow speakers because if Baya was struggling, I assumed they too would be struggling, confused as to what they were to do with this new energy and data space in their brain that they can now begin to put other pieces of their life back in priority.

5HTP isn't going to fix your problem. It's just going to help your serotonin levels get back to normal and from there, you can begin to recover.

It is a weird sensation to go from such a blinding high that is a TEDx talk and then the next day, it's over.

Life goes back to normal. Everyone goes back to the daily routine of their lives and with that there's sadness.

There's a sadness knowing also that you might never get that high ever again.

This is why you see addiction tendencies in celebrities and athletes: we're so used to the high that we can't handle the comedown, so we turn to drugs and alcohol to avoid that silence.

Be prepared for this when you give your TEDx talk.

The next days are going to be brutal as you come off the high.

Chapter 28
Pre-Marketing and Post-Marketing

My pre-marketing plan before my TEDx talk was to begin researching all the podcasts, bloggers and Reddit channels that covered religion, psychology, cult mentality, polygamy, etc.

I made vast excel spreadsheets and gathered as much information as I could. And then I began putting out feelers to all those contacts, announcing I would be giving a TEDx talk that might interest their audience.

Many people responded back.

We planned to time our interviews leading up to the online release of my talk, which I vaguely could tell them would be within a month of my talk, which was on September 17, 2016.

I had dozens of interviews lined up and ready to launch to help get the word out on my talk.

And I also had the NBA D-League website release an article about it, even before I gave the talk. Furthermore, the Ogden Standard Examiner, where I played college basketball at Weber State, released an article about it a month in advance, generating awareness for my old fans at Weber to be on the lookout for it.

Granted, I know all of you do not have the background story that I have, and the network of media outlets I've built up as a professional basketball player around the world. But you can still research bloggers and podcasters that cover your topic.

Remember, bloggers and podcasters are desperate for content! If your talk is even remotely close their general topic, pretty good chance you will get an invite!

Yet, I can credit a vast majority of my success to those outlets that helped me promote my talk: NBA, ESPN, USA Today. It is hard to say with any certainty where the major burst of views stemmed from.

Around a month before my talk, I reached out to my contacts in the media world, be it local newspaper also USA Today, NBA, Bleacher Report, ESPN, letting them know that I going to be giving a TEDx talk, and I was the first NBA player to ever be doing so; something fresh for them to write about.

I have strong contacts in the media and they have always liked me as I've always done a good job of giving them stories. Yes, this is part vanity. But you have to realize news reporters have to give out new content. Their job is on the line every day to produce new content.

Knowing this, I wasn't ever going to give them clichéd answers as an athlete, *"Oh well, all we can do is take it one game at a time, one day at a time, blah blah, etc. etc."*

That's not what news reporters need. They need fresh original content to get to their editor and their readers.

Because I knew this, I always developed a strong relationship with reporters wherever I played and so they were happy to always throw me a bone/favor back if I ever asked of them. And what better time to call in a favor than to announce a TEDx talk?

I was very clear and methodical, white-board methodical when I made a pre-marketing plan and a post-marketing plan. I did pre-marking just to raise a little bit of awareness but put most of the emphasis on post-marketing as I had a whole domino chain set up to fall into place.

My TEDx talk covered so many facets: from religion, psychology to cult mentality, and basketball to disabilities.

And I had them all covered. And one of the best ways to do this is to get friends to blast it for you, so it doesn't look too self-indulgent, or if you are like me and can find a happy balance, just create an alter-ego account and talk about how awesome your talk is, disguised as someone else.

Go ahead! It's fun. The game of the life. Play it!

I did the alter ego thing a lot from Reddit blasts and Facebook posts on group pages and LinkedIn.

And also with pseudo-Twitter and Instagram accounts, that covered not only polygamy but fans of "Sister Wives" and other polygamist reality TV fan club pages.

It is ridiculous how many followers and fans those polygamist reality TV shows have. And they were easy pickings.

Another obvious lead, is the legions of basketball and NBA fans, pages and chat rooms. I just posted as an alter ego and annoyingly blasted those outlets.

Marketing is everything people.

If you have an issue with it, then you shouldn't be reading this book.

And let's not forget about fan pages and groups that follow TEDx Talks. There are so many out there, on all social media platforms. I knew there were so many facets that my TEDx Talk covered that odds were, most TED fans would be associated or intrigued with one topic and would go listen to it.

Think about all the subjects that your TEDx talk is going to be covering, or even skirting, or hell, just glancing at from across the room. So, many threads.

I had them all lined up and so for the next two weeks before my video was released online, I spent time reaching out to those groups asking them if they could support my talk, when I released it.

I did this. There are other ways you can market; you can find all sorts of advertising opportunities online.

Google AdWords works but is expensive, and also draws a lot of spammers.

You don't want that.

However, it can generate a lot of views if you have the budget and don't care about spammers. But you have to have the right keywords in your title and also the subtitle, to get people to even want to click on it when they are on YouTube watching semi-related content. You can also have placement ads on classified ads or whatever, but that is more mass audience approach and not precise.

Marketing your TEDx talk is about precision, not casting a wide net. Most people, honestly, if you can believe it, still don't know what a "TED Talk" is.

I know this seems unbelievable to us fans of TEDx Talks, but it is true. So, if some junkyard dog is looking at a local online classified ad for a used muffler for his '86 Camaro, chances are, he might not be interested or even know what your ad is about. It doesn't apply to him.

Be laser focused!

Facebook advertising was very influential for me, but is also very, very expensive- even more expensive than Google AdWords. Facebook is the most detailed and customizable with precision targeting, as you can select to have your ad reach only people who like TEDx Talks, or only people who like TEDx talks, and/or people who like NBA, and/or Deaf, etc.

Facebook has very precise marketing.
So I was able to create an ad:
What is your polygamy? TEDx- First Deaf Player in NBA History.
Catchy keywords. People clicked.

That is a very intriguing title advertisement on Facebook. People are going to click on that but again it is very expensive and I only intended to use it until it began to give off the appearance of success, because the illusion or appearance of success begets more success.

That is just the way the world works. Even my good friends on Facebook didn't start watching my talk until they saw that it had over 20k views. Then 100k. Then 500k. Then suddenly it was worth their time to sit down for 13 minutes, even though we were supposedly "friends."

People are fickle and/or have short attention spans. And also, again, not all of my friends have the itching to watch TEDx Talks, but would rather watch videos of kittens taking a bath. Sad but true.

All those things came into play and I had them all lined up so that when my video was released, all the contacts I had ready to go, were systematically emailed on their blogs, podcast, chat rooms, social media, on Twitter accounts, and Instagram accounts. I had a lot of groundwork under my belt, ensuring they would blast my talk.

I did this for awareness. I did this to create a buzz and that's OK.

Marketing is part of the game. I know everyone wants to think *"Oh, my TEDx talk is so good that it will be through word of mouth and carry on its own merit."*

This is not true anymore. Those days are pretty much gone.

Marketing is everything; whether you're a speaker or an entrepreneur or a businessman.

Marketing is everything. Especially online marketing. Whether you beg/force/bribe/intimidate/extort/threaten/seduce people to share your video online, or whether someone on their own free will shares your talk on their Facebook page, the result is the same- awareness.

And I knew with my marketing and unique and salacious title of: *"What is your polygamy?"*: *First deaf N.B.A. player, TEDx*... who wouldn't click on that?

Again, it is all about marketing, positioning and knowing the audience you're trying to reach.

Yes, word of mouth is not entirely dead, but it is in the form of social media now for the most part, at least in regards to TEDx Talks, as TEDx Talks rely majorly on social media people in your network sharing.

But here is the problem with Facebook and even most of social media: It has become very apathetic. Especially in October 2016 when the 2016 election was gearing up and everyone had lost their minds.

I was prepared for this. I knew I was not going to get as much help from my immediate network on social media as I wanted.

Most of friends were too busy posting inflammatory lobs at opposing Trump/Clinton supporters, or posting fake news articles that pose as scientifically researched findings, *"This new paste changes the way your cavities heal!"* or the people who post their co-dependent couple photos of how they workout together and make protein shakes together and just really do everything together, because they need everyone to see just how perfect and happy they are because, really, they are arguing too much and will most likely be breaking up soon, and of course again, the people who post about that cute cat that slides into cereal boxes.

Oh, let's not forget the people like me who post the inspirational/motivational memes.

And then... there are the people who post Breitbart articles. That is just a different strain I don't even know where to begin.

When you consider these classifications, finding the TED fans is pretty hard.

You can understand now when I say social media has become very apathetic, especially those who know you and are close to you- you have to realize that for some people if they support and share your content, it makes people feel like they're not doing anything with their lives.

This is called the "Crab in the Bucket" theory and it is very true.

Even if you have people you consider your friends, don't count on them to share your TEDx Talk.

Note: The majority of Facebook friends who shared my TEDx Talk were the semi-friends and not my closest friends and business associates. Sad but true.

You have to put marketing in your own hands and truly manipulate and target it to the people that will be fascinated with your subject.

I spent hundreds of hours researching, marketing and figuring out where my best listeners were going to come from. And then I also allowed myself to take a breath.

Once I had gathered 30,000 views, I went to the Cleveland Cavaliers social media team and when they saw the success of those initial 30,000 views in just a few days, they were confident to throw me a bone and blast it on social media.
The NBA social media marketing reach is one of the best in the entire world and I was fortunate to have that.

So granted, not everyone is going to have that power behind it. The Cavaliers blasting me on social media helped shoot me up to 100k views in the first week.
And again, success begets more success.

I repeated the same cycle.

"Oh, this talk has 100k views now??? I must be worth my time."

And keep repeating the cycle.

Success begets more success.

Each phase had huge help. It is hard to tell where all my views came from and how much of it was word of mouth, organic shares through social media or people speaking about it over the water cooler at work. Or people seeing it on

Cleveland Cavaliers social media or eventually USA Today. It's hard to tell but it all helps.

People seeing I had 100k views, friends or strangers who are TEDx fans, were now more likely to click on it.

It wasn't until my views hit over 100k views that even many of my very close friends then reached out to me,
"Oh, I finally got around to watching your talk, it was amazing."

It wasn't worth their time to watch until they saw that all these other strangers were watching my talk and they are liking it. It signaled to my friends and more strangers that it must mean that the talk is a good talk. *Lance is actually good?*

As the saying goes, a prophet is never accepted among his own people.

Expect this from your friends and family when you give a TEDx Talk. A prophet is never accepted among his own people.
 So that's why you need to market it outside your sphere of influence and reach all the other groups that have common interests as you and the subject that you're covering.

Once the masses begin to see your value then your immediate friends and family will begin to see your value. That seems very backwards but that's just the way human nature is.

I wasn't surprised but I was saddened by how many of my fellow speaker friends did not endorse or congratulate my TEDx Talk. They didn't share it with their social media followers.

Some even hid behind religion, saying because I talked about polygamy or associated it with the current Church of

Jesus Christ of Latter-day Saints, they felt uncomfortable endorsing my talk. But, really we knew what it was: they were threatened that I was taking off so fast.

There was no need to hide behind religion. Anyone who watches the talk knows that there was nothing to be offended about, unless you are still a practicing polygamist and I am using you as a bat to beat everyone else with. That would sting for a bit, I get it. But no one escapes my talk unscathed. No one.

My fellow speaker friends, who talk a big game about being bold, but hid behind religious sensitivity, could have simply said, *"You know a lot of my followers are religious/Mormon, and if they see me endorsing you talking about polygamy, it will make them uncomfortable and I'm afraid about blowback."*
That would have been more honest. And I could have respected that.

I was disappointed. I wasn't upset or angry but I was disappointed.
I had a lot of fellow speakers who pose tough to their audience, but when it comes to talking about real tough things, taboo things, they play it safe. I was sad, but it also a sign that I had gotten what I wanted, because I wanted to be a different bread of speaker.

The year before when I retired from basketball and told myself I was going to be a motivational speaker, I made a promise to myself and my son that I was always going to walk the talk.
That I was going to set myself apart.
That I was going to be the authentic speaker. That if I was professing to do something on stage, I would better make sure that I was walking the talk and not just being a big game of talk.

With a lot of my fellow speakers distancing themselves from me, it let me know that I had walked the talk- that I had set myself apart.

Of course, now that my TEDx has generated over a million views, some of those same people that distanced themselves from me were suddenly very quick to reach out to congratulate me.

When things are going well, you can always count on your bandwagon friends to jump back on ship. But when it is a gamble, when things are unsure, few people will jump in the wheelbarrow and go across the tightrope with you. This is life.

As November neared, the election of 2016 was a big behemoth that I had to move around, and so I did pause a lot of my hustling for a while until after November 8th, Election Night.

When the election was over, I sent off a series of press releases with my good friend and marketing guide, Dave Murray, to dozens of media outlets, television stations, newspapers, radio stations, announcing that my talk had over two hundred fifty thousand views.

"First deaf player in N.B.A. history TEDx talk goes viral," was the title of the press release.

That's a gripping title, and again people are going to click on that. Those press releases conjured another wave of social media blast to bloggers and podcasters, which began to compound my views very quickly, so that at the end of the second month, I passed 1 million views.

It's all about marketing and it is all about pushing, hustling.

Once we got 500k views, Dave and I did another press release.

750k views? Another press release, and so on and so on.

It is always about showing momentum. About showing success, about putting your best foot forward.

Success begets success.

While social media, on one hand, is not necessarily "real," you can use it correctly as a tool to show success. It helps you gain more success, and more viewers. It gets the word out to people, because that's how people get their news now.

So, with each round of success that I showed, I kept pushing and hustling. It must have been and most likely was annoying to people that already knew about my TEDx talk. Even if they were kind of "over it," I was going to keep pushing and reaching more and more people.

And I will continue to do so, probably until I die. Because my message, I believe in my heart, is for everyone.

Everyone.

Success begets success. Build momentum and keep building on that momentum: That's all that marketing is and marketing is everything

Chapter 29
Goodbye

As I close, haven given you all of this information, a question must be asked:

If my talk hadn't reached a million views, would it still have been a good talk?

Answer: Absolutely.

The quality and message of my talk, for me, is not measured by the number of views it receives. Views are simply business. It has nothing to do to with the heart and soul of "What is your Polygamy?"

I am more proud of that talk, than I am of my NBA resume. Truly. That talk was a weaving of the many patterns of my life that have come flowing together, and I was able to create a tapestry that tells a story that is for anybody. My story is your story. It is everyone's story.

I hope that as you work, struggle and persevere to finally getting your moment on the stage, whether or not your talk gets a million views, that you allow yourself that same compassion and clarity.

Your TEDx talk is not attached to the viewership outcome.

But more importantly…

Your self-worth is never attached to an outcome.

Best of luck for the incredible journey you are embarking on, for a TEDx talk is not a destination or end result- it is a journey of self-discovery.

And on that journey, always choose clarity. And always choose to move in gratitude.

Always function from your authentic space, and I promise you, you cannot fail.

Part Two
Partners and Mentors

"Awakening the Roaring Lion"
Dennis Allen, MBA

I, TOO, WAS DREAMING WHILE OTHERS SLEPT

I, too, was dreaming while others slept.
Dreaming dreams wide awake instead of sleep.
Working, toiling through the night,
Creating the hopes and dreams inside of me

Tired, yes, yet still I tried, and tried, and tried
And crafted my dreams with open eyes
While others slept, I chose to dream
Late into the night-- early into the morning.

Call it effort, call it work, call it will
Call it persistence, not talent or skill.
Call it courage or call it grit.
Call it my dream because I created it.

I, too, was dreaming while others slept.
I gave my all, my best, I never quit.
So, now awake I live my dream.
I am now what I had hoped to be.

I, too, was dreaming while others slept.
Dreaming dreams wide awake instead of sleep.
Working, toiling through the night,
Creating the hopes and dreams inside of me.

(Dennis Allen)
....

I love big dreams. I love making conditions favorable for people to live their big dreams.

Igniting a powerful energy from within and crafting practical plans for making the big dream a reality, brings me great joy. I love courageous empowerment and inner joy in all their many forms.

In my labor of love of helping people dream big dreams and envision themselves in those dreams, there are many moments behind the scenes, which are not as shiny and sexy as the actual on-stage performance or finished product.

Those moments are the quiet moments when it seems no one is watching. The kind of moments where as a person we test our resolve and our deep courage and grit from within. Will we stay true to our dream? Will we put in our effort and very best no matter what? Will we do whatever work is necessary to achieve our goals?

So, what are the backstage moments for giving a million view TEDx talk or for achieving any noble goal for that matter? How did Lance get over 2.5 million views on YouTube and why is that beneficial or helpful to know?

Backstage moments are often skipped over because they seem like simple things repeated again and again in strategic areas. The backstage moments can be thought of as the explanation of how the magician did the trick.

Sometimes we don't want to really know, but it is significant to understand or be familiar with the notion that there is generally always some sort of backstage moment and work in the achievement of any excellent thing.

The work may come from specific thoughts or emotions, it may come from specific action tasks. Sometimes it is nice to think that stuff just magically appears, but the reality is magical thinking is not the complete story. More often than not, there is a fair amount of doing and applied effort.

Backstage moments are often dusty, sweaty, and hot back-breaking everyday moments of solid training with sincere effort. They are moments of living-breathing courage and grit in action. These everyday moments can also be filled with joy in the journey. Amid progress and small wins, these moments are also often filled with stumbles, falls, and failures.

We can choose to quit and give up or we can choose to rise and get up again and again as many times as necessary. We train and we prepare. We improve our skills and our confidence. We get better. These interesting moments where we test our true integrity are the moments which springboard our dreams and launch us forward to the closer realization of our amazing potential. It seems after these moments where we truly test our resolve to achieve our goal--then arrives the other moments-- those moments where we easily and effortlessly make magic happen. Our honed talents shine in a more polished and powerful manner. We draw crowds of followers to watch us. We live in the spotlight. Our actions seem to flow in a timeless, beautiful way.

Often the work and effort can be challenging and uncomfortable, but I love doing dream work myself and seeing others do their own dream work-- the actual doing part. I am honored and inspired by the noble courage, grit, effort, and persistence in making big dreams happen and achieving big dream goals. Something about that brings me unspeakable joy and helps me be a better person.

"I'm possible" and "impossible" are essentially the same word--the only difference is creating space and placing a tiny mark which represents I am.

Lance Allred is one of the most remarkable individuals I know. He brings an energy of authentic credibility and genuineness to situations. It seems to be a natural result of his humble confidence and sincere choice for leadership, courage, and grit.

When I met Lance, he was transitioning out of his professional basketball career. He was also going through a challenging divorce. He had big dream goals, yet he was stuck. Lance was giving his all, but in that challenging season in his life, Lance felt broken and was sincerely looking for ways to authentically move past the roadblocks. I write and share this only because Lance has given me permission to share. This is the kind of person Lance is--open, honest, and genuine.

From the outside, to a casual observer, Lance appeared to be very successful. A young good-looking, near 7-foot tall former professional NBA basketball player who played with LeBron James on the Cavaliers. I first met Lance at the Cottonwood Country Club in Salt Lake City through a mutual friend.

In the moment I met Lance, I liked him. We became fast friends. In our first encounter, I saw Lance for who he was and who he was not. I trusted Lance and yet could clearly discern, behind the front he was showing, there were some deeper hurts and challenging issues going on. I could feel the pain and hurt hidden deep within--not because I am some new age mind reader -- I simply could understand and empathize because I too had been there before. My heart went out to him. Lance definitely had built up his walls to defend himself from real or imagined attackers. I saw past his walls to the true, noble and great person Lance truly is.

"He drew a circle that shut me out, heretic, rebel, thing to flout--but love and I had the wit to win, we drew a circle and took him in." (Edwin Markham)

In our first meeting together, we discussed some seemingly lucrative business deals in the education and technology space which could powerfully transform the lives of thousands of people in positive ways. I shared with Lance some of my previous experiences, attempts, and efforts integrating of this technology into the existing business model with a fortune 100 company -- a potential $50 million per year value creation deal. Lance discussed some of his connections, efforts, and intention to bring this to a large university -- a potential $800,000 per month value creation deal. We discussed our experiences working the current CEO of the tech company, a former Olympic Athlete.

After our first meeting, Lance invited me to one of his speaking events. I went and saw Lance speak to a large audience of university students and staff at a local university. Candidly his speaking was OK, but his message was a little muddled, and I thought he could use some help. (Obviously this has changed-- Lance is an EXCELLENT speaker and presenter, besides his 2.5+ million TEDx Talk on YouTube, Lance is one of the foremost sought after keynote speakers in the country.)

Sometimes I can see clearly for others that which they cannot see for themselves just yet. As humans we are often blind to our own greatness and potential. Sometimes we settle--not knowing what we don't know. We simply accept at face value or often buy into the false misperceptions, inaccurate judgements of people around us. We far too often maintain the status quo and keep ourselves in the dark far below our full potential and brilliant shiny true selves.

For as tall as he was, big Lance was stuck in being small. Lance had noble aspirations and more than anything he wanted to break free to the next stage and season of his life of living his dream to its full potential. I could see it. I could sense it. However, until Lance chose to ask me for help and invite me in, all I could do was just be in neutral awareness as an outside observer.

Lance invited me into his world. We exchanged authentic conversations about hopes, dreams, and vulnerabilities. I shared with Lance my journey, challenges, and setbacks.

Lance shared with me his current situation and where he wanted to go. I agreed to help make it happen.

Lance hired me as his executive coach. He wanted to do a TEDx talk and do it incredibly well. I agreed and we went to work. I did not reduce my coaching fee. Lance paid full price. We did get creative on how the payment for the full coaching fee was paid and did a customized in-kind, fair-trade value exchange.

Lance worked his tail off. He spent countless hours and late nights doing the work required to create a powerful presentation. He humbly accepted feedback and help. Lance stayed true to his big vision goal and dream. I freely gave Lance full permission to use my materials and insights in his presentation and encouraged him to mix it with his own experiences and own his presentation 100 percent.

Lance must have had it easy, right? Things probably came really easy for Lance which made it super easy for him to give a million view TEDx Talk, right? Yes, maybe so. Maybe the conditions were absolutely perfect for Lance to tap into his authentic voice and receive powerful momentum to make his dreams a reality? Perhaps the challenges and setbacks worked very well in Lance's favor because he willed it so?

Let's talk about what those conditions looked like at the time. If Lance wanted to play the victim or wanted to use his situation for an excuse, he certainly could have done so easily and justified why he could not pursue his goal. You name the excuse most people use and yes--very likely that excuse was readily available for Lance.

When I met Lance, he was sleeping on the floor in a tiny basement room of a family member's home. It was a small, average-sized home. Lance barely had enough room for himself let alone his 2 year old son.

In time Lance began to see and believe in his true self and in doing so nudged forward. Lance upgraded his sleeping arrangements to a broken second-hand leather couch from a local thrift shop. It was certainly not a luxurious California king bed, but it was a step up from sleeping on the floor. The couch would not fit into the basement in one piece. To make it work, the couch was cut with a saw and jerry-rigged reassembled back together in order to finagle the furniture into the tiny room in corner. The couch was perhaps a little bit better than the cold hard floor, but Lance's feet still hung off the end. Definitely not the most comfortable rest and certainly not the most helpful situation for aching backs.

Lance made more progress and created more opportunities. Lance chose to move to a new place. He made conditions favorable to make it so. Lance worked hard and found a suitable location. It wasn't a big place, but it was his place with the needed space. I showed up and helped Lance move to his new apartment and place of his own with room for his son. By relative comparison this was a mansion or castle compared to Lance's Harry Potter closet under the stairs.

We were exhilarated and thrilled to dump Lance's old leather couch he'd been sleeping on. I think that was super meaningful for Lance and represented a major milestone and a closed chapter of that season of his life.

What is your figurative old couch to dump and get rid of? What things do you want to let go of to make room for something new and better?

For Lance's new place, I donated a beautiful handcrafted wooden kitchen table which I had purchased from my grandfather and grandmother. I also freely gave Lance a washer and dryer. I donated a bunch of kitchen items and food. I showed up with a trailer and jeep to be there and help. I gave and served because others did that for me at a similar sort of challenging season in my own life. I jumped with delight at opportunity to pay forward the abundant compassion and kindness I had received. This was a definite joy bringer for me. Lance and I worked hard moving his stuff. I will never forget the moment after the long day of moving. Sigh... That look in Lance's face, the quivering voice of heartfelt gratitude and appreciation---I felt like I was looking in the mirror at myself back in time when I was in a similar situation. "Thank you Dennis, thank you. You have no idea." Tears flowed down his face. It's always something cool to see a big man cry. For the record, I cried, too.

Lance has been on a tough journey and has chosen to rise to the challenge the very best he can no matter the situation. Lance has chosen to allow his setbacks to help move him forward. He has gracefully moved forward with every season in his life.

Please, do not misunderstand what I am saying. I believe that there is perfection in every step of the journey. Lance was absolutely perfect, exactly how he was and was not in that moment, stage, and season in his life. Much like how a rose is perfect in every stage and season from a new tiny seedling, small blossom, full-bloom rose, or mature end-of-season plant.

The story of Lance's life and interesting journey has inspired me in many, many ways. I will always appreciate his determination and effort. I like Lance just as he was then, as he is right now, and how he will be in the future. I like Lance in every stage of his development and progression.

I, too, am perfect exactly as I am, and as I am not. That doesn't mean I don't continually seek to improve and constantly stretch myself outside my comfort zone. It just means I am okay being me right now in this moment. I have chosen for myself as a lifestyle choice, courageous empowerment, ongoing improvement, and the energetic quest of inner joy.

I hope to always be the first one to raise my hand to candidly admit I have many flaws and many unrealized dreams. I have many weaknesses, shortcomings, and areas under-construction and needing improvement. I make many mistakes and have my own share of naysayers and critics. I have fought many battles and have lost many times. The most I can do is my best.

Somehow I still choose to pick myself up and humbly and confidently move forward the best I can with whatever I can. I believe a healthy dose of confident humility, approachable authenticity, sincere honesty, and a bit of humor seems to help make friends. I found an endless renewable energy resource in humor by learning to laugh at my endless parade of errors, quirks, and vulnerabilities. Lance has lifted me and helped me in many different ways, and I will always be grateful for his friendship and example.

Some people have wondered how did the title of the TEDx talk come about? In a coaching conversation we had together, Lance received a powerful "Ah-ha" moment of brilliant illumination. Lance was concerned about how to make his weird story relatable to people, and I remember telling Lance, "Your story is not all that different from anyone else. Seriously you are more relatable to so many people more than you might imagine. Everybody, and I mean everybody, has some sort of past blueprint of mental and emotional patterns that keeps them where they are. Maybe it is Polygamy? Maybe it is poverty? Maybe it is relationships, weight loss, work, sports, or something else? Everybody has their own version of their own sort of "Polygamy" in one form or another. What is your polygamy? Everybody is looking for courage, grit, leadership, and perseverance to move beyond where they might be stuck to get themselves to a better place. Everybody has areas in their lives they are not even aware could perhaps be better. Maybe that's really what you are looking to do- to connect with others and raise their awareness of to a better version of themselves. Maybe ask what is their polygamy? What's my polygamy? What's your polygamy?"

Lance loved that.

I was so proud of Lance after his talk. The joy in seeing him step into his full stature on stage was beyond words. When Lance's TEDx talk went live on YouTube I was about the 7th view of it. I shared it with my friends and family and my network of influence. Within about a month or two Lance had over 200,000 views. A little while later Lance received over 1 million views on his talk. Soon after 2.5 million views. There is something deeply meaningful for me to think of a deaf kid, born in a polygamous commune, with a terrible speech impediment, who underwent years and years of speech therapy to not only make it to play in NBA as a professional basketball player, but to stand on a major platform and give a powerful presentation to the world. Wow.

I believe an essential part of achieving success is simply stepping outside our comfort zones; creating practical plans for allowing the excuses to be let go; and nudging ourselves a little bit closer to our hoped-for big dream goal. This sort of stuff requires leadership, perseverance, and grit. First comes a fierce loyalty to the dream which must stay through the entire pursuit. Next comes the practical step-by-step processes and plans which sort of emerge with the momentum of moving forward.

So, how does one give a million view TEDx talk? I believe first and foremost is "you gotta want it!" You need to choose to create that and fiercely commit to it. When you make your definite decision to make it happen, you simply follow through and do whatever it takes to make it so. The first step is clear and definite commitment. This is the leadership and boldness initiative of chutzpah also known as the courage step. The next piece is the follow-through and perseverance. This is the grit step.

In my book, "Strong Thanks Courage of the Wholehearted" I wrote a chapter on the Butterfly Ripple Effect, and shared an excerpt from W.H. Murray's 1951, Scottish Himalayan Expedition, "But when I said that nothing had been done, I erred in one important matter. We had definitely committed ourselves and were halfway out of our ruts. We had put down our passage money--booked a sailing to Bombay. This may sound too simple, but is great in consequence. Until one is committed there is hesitancy, the chance to draw back, always ineffectiveness. Concerning all acts of initiative (and creation), there is one elementary truth the ignorance of which kills countless ideas and splendid plans: that the moment one definitely commits oneself, then providence moves too. A whole stream of events issues from the decision, raising in one's favor all manner of unforeseen incidents, meetings, and material assistance, which no man could have dreamt would have come his way. I learned a deep respect for one of Goethe's couplets: Whatever you can do or dream you can do, begin it. Boldness has genius, power, and magic in it!"

Just what are the comfort zone or boundaries we stay within? What exactly are those invisible mental and emotional walls we surround ourselves with as a powerful forcefield? We all have them--that is if we choose to be humble enough to openly acknowledge that we don't know everything about everything.

Many of us choose status quo complacency, above moving beyond our comfort zones, a little into the unknown and unskilled areas of our lives. We fear the unknown. We fear some elusive judgemental ghost called "they". What would "they" say? What would "they" think if I failed? "They" might laugh at me or ridicule me for trying. "They" might think I'm crazy to leave my cozy comfort zone.

Far too many of us are talented and gifted beyond compare and live far, far, far below our full potential.

As humans we are all naturally gifted and talented and that often comes in greater strength and demonstration as we seemingly, unnaturally persevere beyond our comfort zones, work our asses off, and show up again and again and again through blood, sweat and tears. The combination of raw talent, courage and grit is powerful and formidable.

What is your polygamy? What is your courage and grit? Perhaps the journey begins by asking interesting and powerful questions and then being open to consider the possibilities?

How exactly do we learn to choose to rise again after we fall? What is that deep power from within which brings us to our feet again and again?

In practical terms, how does one enter that arena of courage and grit with that palpable swagger of confidence and energizing passion for the sport? How do we become legendary and create a profound life-changing positive legacy for others to enjoy and follow after?

Perhaps the secret is we simply choose to do our best effort and to show up roaring like a lion?

I saw within Lance a noble and fierce lion. A powerful and roaring lion. Lance reminded me of my dear friend Dov Siporin, who did the impossible again and again. Dov beat the odds--the crazy odds which were stacked against him. He chose to bring love, humor, and life to every precious moment he could. He broke past all the limits and expectations. My friend Dov courageously battled terminal cancer for years, well beyond a time frame the doctors gave him to live. Dov left behind a wife and two small children as well as a legacy of courage which has positively influenced thousands in meaningful ways. Dov wrote a powerful poem which served as a bookend to his inspiring life. Dov would approve of me sharing it here because it fits to bookend this chapter.

MY HOPE

My hope is not footsteps on the beach,
Nor a life-jacket tossed to my awaiting arms.
My hope is not a promise after the storm.
My hope does not whisper sweet things,
It does not lead me gently through pain,
Through suffering.
It is not grace, it is not beauty,
It is not sweetness, it is not light.
No,
My hope is a dirty thing
His lip split open, his eye swollen shut
He is covered in bruises, old and new.
My hope fights in the mud, in the shit,
Knuckles raw,
Sweat running down his face.
My hope stands with me
In the gutter and growls.
My hope is covered in scars,
His bones have broken and mended
And broken again.
My hope laughs at me when I give up,
When I surrender, he's been through too
Damn much, he knows me better.
My hope gets up, again and again
And again.
And in the night, in the dark
My hope smiles, My hope swears,
My hope spits blood, clenches his fits
And my hope... My hope roars.
(Dov Siporin)

- Dennis Allen, MBA
Executive Coach
and Author

"Planes and Train...wrecks"
Christoph Merrill

As a Professional Speaker you spend a lot of time, on a lot of airplanes. You learn the art and science of "plane talk." The old, "Where you headed? Going for Business or Pleasure? What do you do for a living?"

You know the Plane Talk I am talking about, right?

On one flight, I noticed that the woman next to me had her wedding ring on the wrong finger. I couldn't help myself, I had to know why, So I said, "I noticed that your wedding ring is on the wrong finger, can I ask you why?

She looked at me and calmly replied, "It's because I married the wrong man."

Now I have NO idea if she did or did not, but it made me think that most people have the wrong idea about what it takes to be a successful speaker, what success even is, and how their success affects the lives of others.

So, my goal is to Motivate, to Inspire, and to give you that little extra "kick" when you need it the most. My goal is to have you remember just one thing, yep, only one thing. Keep reading to figure out what that one thing is; if you do, you will be a better person, a better lover and a significantly better speaker.

There are four basic reasons why most people are not successful. It is really quite simple; see, most people do not have "any" goals.

Reason one: they have not been sold on "why" they should have goals. Yes, I did say "Sold." Now, I will sell you.

I will "sell" you on "the why" you must have goals to become a successful speaker. Did you notice, just there, I did not say, "I hope to, or I plan on, or I will try to sell you."

No, I said "I Will", and I will.

Reason two: most people have No idea how to set goals. So, I will give you a simple formula for setting your goals, that if you follow the formula, you will accelerate your success in life, as well as a speaker.

Reason three: fear. See, there is risk involved when you say "I'm going to do…" whatever it is. This happens, even if you do not even tell another soul about the goal. Whenever you set a goal, there's a certain amount of risk, at least risk to your EGO involved.

Finally, reason four: most speakers have "Imposter Syndrome." This is because they have a poor self-image.

If you do not think you deserve success, if you do not think you deserve a standing ovation, to be a million–views speaker, to have a message worth sharing; if you don't think you deserve them, then you will do all the things that will keep you from getting them.

Let's break them down, using Lance as the guinea pig, cool? Cool!

When I met Lance he wasn't "sold" on what his "goal" was for his speech. He had a bunch of things going for him. He was 6'11", he's deaf, and he played in the NBA, oh and he was a polygamist kid.

But, the first time I heard Lance speak, it was a train-wreck, and for good reason. I had no interest in listening. None, his message did not relate to me. I will never be 6'11." I am not deaf, nor do I hope to be. And I have no desire to play in the NBA, and I can't imagine ever being a polygamist, I have my hands full with one wife, let alone two or ten, wozza, no thanks!

See, his message was ALL about him and "his" story. He did not have any "goals" for his speech, I am sure he had hope to inspire, to motivate, to do whatever it was. He didn't. Lance was not "sold" on "his why, his goal" for the speech, therefore, his message was lost, it did not connect.

Lance wasn't sure how to set the goals for his speech, and it showed. The simple formula I gave him to use to Accelerate the Success of his message was this:

Step 1 – Clearly define a Theme, I call it "The one memory" – This is the first "goal". If your audience walks out and only has "one" memory about your speech, it should be your "Why"? This MUST be relatable to your audience, that's the "why." If this doesn't happen, you didn't sell them on why they should care.

Step 2 – Follow the recipe – Great cakes don't just happen, and neither do speeches. If you want to "just give a speech" then that's all it will be, given, thrown together, but if you want to create a memorable message, you have to create a recipe to follow. What recipe am I referring to? Yours, you must craft your own original recipe.

Step 3 – Practice, Refine, Practice More – Give your speech to any and everyone who will listen, ask them one question: what is the one thing you remember? If it isn't "The One Memory", rewrite it and keep giving it until at least 20 people all remember, "the One Thing."

Step 4 – "Be ALL In" – Once you have defined a theme, practiced, refined and practiced some more, and you have created your own recipe; Set a date, the date you will deliver your speech to a live audience. Go for it. Own it!

Lance was full of fear, and not the kind you think of when you typically think of, stage fright of public speaking which for most people is the number one fear.

Rather, Lance fearful of being vulnerable.

See his original speech was chalk full of "facts" which isn't bad, but when it's full of all "facts" and very little "emotion" the message is lost.

Because of Lance's personal experiences with his "message" he was afraid to be vulnerable, to show true emotion. The audience has what I call a "sniff – sniff" meter, they have all seen enough "speakers" to determine quickly if they are full of it or not. To truly connect with any audience, you must be authentic, real and vulnerable. No one is perfect, so stop trying to be.

Lastly, everyone suffers from Imposter Syndrome, at some point in his or her speaking career. Everyone does. If they say they don't, they probably lie about a lot of other things too.

Here's the deal, you either embrace you talents or your don't. You either embrace your challenges or you don't. You either accept that you have something to share that someone needs to hear, or yep, you guessed it, you don't.

If you let yourself believe you do not deserve success, then you are only hurting those who need to hear your message.

The biggest reason I offered to help Lance, was one thing-he was humble enough to do it.

See a lot of aspiring speakers ask for help, but they don't follow the advice given. Lance certainly did.

He had to do the heavy lifting, and as you have seen, he knocked it out of the park. I'm proud to call Lance a friend.

- Christoph Merrill
Motivational Speaker
and Trainer

152

"Discovering Clarity"
Christy Foster

Lance and I grew up in the same place in rural Montana, but this chapter isn't about polygamy. Just as any insightful person knows his talk wasn't really about polygamy either. Nor is this chapter about Lance's journey from Montana to the NBA. This chapter is about his journey in understanding his mind-body-spirit connection.

When I first began working with Lance he came to me for joint pain that would not go away, no matter what he tried. You might assume that joint pain for a professional athlete would indicate years of wear and overuse had taken a toll on the body.

However, in Lance's case, the joint pain would not respond to normal therapy usually associated with athletic injuries. He had the best therapists available to him, yet was unable to gain consistent relief from his joint pain. There seemed to be another root cause to his discomfort, *a missing piece to the puzzle of his pain.*

As a Psychosomatic Therapist, I help clients bring balance to the relationship between the mind and the physical body. When I see a client for the first time, they usually come to me because they have a physical ailment that other modalities or therapies have not been able to fully address. For example, people who may experience persistent headaches, back pain, insomnia, and neck pain are great candidates for this type of therapy. Some of these individuals try for years to overcome their physical pain with no avail. Lance was one of these patients who could not overcome his chronic discomfort.

Figuring out why someone is not healing is a process of looking at the system as a whole, through analysis on a physical and emotional level. Candace B. Pert, neuroscientist, describes our whole system as a psychosomatic information network. Through her years of research, she found that physiology and emotions are inseparable. She explains, "When stored or blocked emotions are released through touch or other physical methods, there is a clearing of our internal pathways, which we experience as energy. By getting in touch with our emotions, both by listening to them and by directing them through the psychosomatic network, we gain access to the healing wisdom that is everyone's natural biological right."

It is this internal "healing wisdom" that Lance set out to discover.

I begin work with my clients by having them fill out an intake form which includes a physical history: Heart or circulatory problems, high or low blood pressure, diabetes, operations, injuries, accidents, broken bones, and any other diseases.

Then we take an in-depth look at the history and emotions of their life. We discuss memories from childhood like a broken arm, moving to a new city, or even falling out of a tree. We talk about adolescence and the issues and challenges that may have come with their teenage years. We reflect on adulthood which brings yet more challenges: Starting a career, relationships and possibly marriage, buying a first home, or starting a family.

This chronological and emotional history helps inform a client's physical history. Pert's research has given us a new understanding of the power of our minds and our feelings to directly and profoundly affect our health and well-being. She explains, "Bodymind medicine is based on the recognition of the relationship between mind and body, the body's innate healing potential, and the partnership of patient and healer in restoring the body to health."

Lance's physical and emotional history gave insight into his pain that would not respond to other treatments.

By the age of 5, Lance was experiencing the frustration of not being able to communicate with his family circle; his deafness had also created a severe speech impediment. He couldn't hear the voices of his family very well, and they were not able to understand what he was telling them.

Years and years went by for Lance as he felt the isolation of not understanding or being understood by those around him. The frustration Lance felt as a very young boy followed him into adolescence and adulthood. Can you imagine the annoyance he must have gone through with friends, teachers, and coaches? His ability to function as an elite level athlete and have the disability of being deaf is truly miraculous. He practiced and practiced for years to be understood through hard work and sheer willpower. But scars remained.

Deb Shapiro, meditation and mindfulness expert, explains in her book, *Your Body Speaks Your Mind,* that joint issues may be connected to the expression of your feelings through your movements, and any conflict you may be experiencing with those feelings will be apparent.

She goes on to explain how inflammation of the joints may be an indication that a person is unable to move or flow with life. There can be a feeling of stuckness or an inability to express deeper feelings.

Our bodies and minds are one system. Someone--like Lance--experiencing joint pain may be feeling misunderstood and have a feeling of becoming stiff or unable to move. Tension in the joints may indicate someone with a very strong mind and someone who is extremely determined to hold their ground. When Lance gained a better understanding of the emotional and physical relationship of his body, it allowed him to begin the process of letting go of his past. He became clear in his mind and more accepting of himself.

When I watched Lance deliver his TEDx Talk, "What Is Your Polygamy?" I felt such a sense of contentment for Lance and what he's discovered along his journey and the parallels I've seen in my own journey.

Notice how Lance, in his TEDx Talk, was open emotionally--through his words, and open physically--through his body language? Lance is an authentic speaker who continues to examine and come to terms with his emotional history. Lance speaks with authenticity and integrity rooted in his emotional awareness. Other speakers may hide their emotions behind their words, never allowing the audience to see their true self, this is not the case with Lance.

The moment he said, "Love is unconditional or it is not love at all" is a powerful moment. The unconditional love Lance talks about is an unconditional love that comes from within him first. As Lance chooses to be a leader in his own life, and as he teaches others to practice the mindful act of changing their language to reflect their own leadership, he continues healing through all levels of his Mind-Body-Spirit.

Despite all the challenges life has presented him, Lance continues to choose clarity.

- Christy Foster
  Psychosomatic
  Therapist

"Anatomy of a TEDx Talk"

or

"How a Deaf Kid from a Polygamist Commune Scored BIG on YouTube"

David K Brake

When a deaf kid from a polygamous compound in Montana navigates some of the most bizarre obstacles life can toss at you, there's a compelling story to be told. When the same kid grows into a 6'11" man and makes it to the National Basketball Association to become the first deaf player in league history and then plays alongside the legendary Lebron James and his Cleveland Cavaliers, the story becomes something else entirely, something Horatio Alger would have sold his soul to tell.

Horatio is not here to tell that story, but it turns out the deaf kid, Lance Allred, is pretty good at telling his own story. In fact, he's had over 2.7 million views of his TEDx talk, a pretty impressive achievement itself.

So how did Lance score so many views in a relatively short period of time? Well, that's the story I'm here to tell.

Lance Allred is a practitioner of the **ACCESS Model**, a content development and marketing strategy anyone can use to ideate, validate, and promote their story, business, or expertise. And like almost everything else he does, he's good at it.

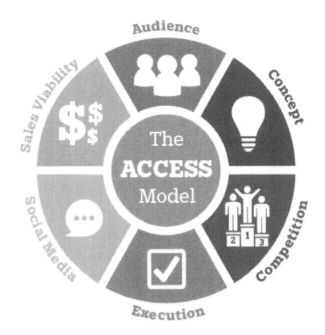

ACCESS starts with AUDIENCE

Turns out your 11th grade English teacher was right. You need to know your audience. Once you know your audience, you can craft your story or presentation around the attributes of that audience.

Here's what Lance knows about the typical TED audience:

- Average age = 41
- Mean Household Income = $100,000
- 51% Male
- 49% Female
- 81% are college graduates
- 47% work in the C-Suite of their companies

- They have a strong Social Media presence

It helped that his talk was delivered at TEDxSaltLakeCity. He was able to tap into cultural cross-talk around the topic of polygamy, something he obviously knows a lot about. Outside of Utah polygamy is mysterious and perverse. Within the state, there's a finer distinction of what polygamy is and how it manifests itself. The Mormons (officially, The Church of Jesus Christ of Latter-day Saints) used to do it, but reject it now. Some splinter groups still do it, and boldly proclaim their allegiance to it. Other splinter groups do it but do their best to hide it. There are more than 60,000 practicing polygamists in Utah and surrounding states, so whether you reject it, rejoice over it, or really don't talk about it, it's one of the state's dirty little secrets. And audiences everywhere love dirty little secrets.

Lance's CONCEPT

Once you have your sights on the right audience, you need to ideate and validate a good concept. A concept is the foundation that your content is built upon. Because Lance's worldview and competitive nature don't allow him to blame his challenges on life's hurdles, he doesn't see being deaf and a victim of a polygamous cult as an excuse to underachieve. Were he wired differently, he might choose to blame others, but that's not Lance.

In an epiphanous moment some time ago, Lance realized that as extraordinary as his challenges might seem to others, everybody actually has challenges. And we all have different abilities to handle these challenges. In a strange, counterintuitive way, we all have our own "polygamy" that shadows us through life, ready to hold us down or back.

159

Thus, a concept was born: **What's Your Polygamy?** Lance could tell his colorful story in a context that made other people think about the things that keep them from achieving success. Armed with this concept, Lance tested and iterated it with a few audiences until he knew he had something.

Knowing the COMPETITION

Not surprisingly there are other TEDx Talks on polygamy and several of its closest cousins, polygyny, polyandry, bigamy, and monogamy. There are books, movies, and YouTube videos. Surprisingly, there's a lot of polygamy-related content.

Lance scanned the digital shelves of Amazon.com and searched the YouTube archives to see if anyone was presenting the "dirty little secret" as he intended to present it. Nothing really surfaced. It hit him though, that the theme of his talk was not really polygamy. It was about overcoming obstacles and realizing one's potential. There's A LOT of content out there that falls into that category. Polygamy, it turned out, was a colorful vehicle for delivering that message.

Other people used drugs, alcohol, gambling, eating disorders, and numerous other human afflictions as their vehicle for talking about success and overcoming obstacles. These things were to them what polygamy was to Lance. Not surprisingly, Lance was able to craft a provocative title, *What's Your Polygamy?*

This title put him right in middle of the pack of authors and speakers who focus on success and achievement, a crowded but popular space to be sure. But polygamy gave him an edge.

Being legally deaf made that edge sharp. Fighting his way into the NBA became the thing that made him and his TEDx talk totally unique. It's pretty safe to say that Lebron James had never had a locker next to a 6'11" deaf kid from a polygamous commune in Montana, and as good a picture as that creates in your mind, the story of how Lance got there is what makes his TEDx Talk resonate with so many people.

It's All About EXECUTION

Lance knows that potential means nothing without execution. He worked hard to build his TEDx Talk around the concept of *What's Your Polygamy?* He curated stories, photographs, video clips, and artifacts that supported his theme, and then he assembled them into a meaningful package that enhanced the theme.

All good talks, TEDx Talks or otherwise, are influenced by body language, physical movement across and through space, and the instrumental application of one's voice. It's the upward vocal lilt when asking a question to your audience, the dramatic pause as you tee up the answer, and the lowered voice giving gravitas to the words that follow, that make your talk as unique as a fingerprint.

Lance practiced this, sought feedback, and iterated it until he reached the "Goldilocks Moment" where he was confident that it was "just right" for his audience.

SOCIAL MEDIA is a Maven

Lance knows that the TED brand is powerful. Or, in the words of The New Yorker, "TED has created a product that's sophisticated, popular, lucrative, socially conscious, and wildly pervasive."

TED's social media footprint includes:

- 8.7 million Facebook friends
- 7.8 million Twitter followers
- 1.6 million connections on LinkedIn

It's fair to say that just about any talk that gets the TED or TEDx brand attached to it will get more attention because of the brand. But that's not to take anything away from Lance's own social media strategy.

Lance has an active presence on social media, and he uses it to carefully position and promote his own *Thought Leadership*. That's right, Lance is a thought leader. Not a thought leader on polygamy. Not even a thought leader on basketball. Lance is a thought leader when it comes to personal motivation, success in life, leadership, and management.

He uses his social media content, whether original, curated, or shared/recommended to stay connected with his social networks and professional communities. It's not always easy. It kind of reminds him of basketball practice: you do it almost everyday until it becomes second nature. Social media has become part of Lance's daily routine.

As thought leadership reaches a highpoint, your influence with friends and colleagues increases, your recommendations mean more, your feedback becomes sought-after and valuable. Odd as the analogy might seem, you become the trusted village maven whose friends and neighbors would go to her for advice, recommendations, and connections to people who could help them with whatever they needed.

Consumer Behavior expert Dr. Linda Price coined the term "Market Maven" to describe those people in our society who have earned the trust of their "villages" and wield considerable influence within their communities. Why? Because information is their expertise. So whether you're looking for a restaurant recommendation or the best deal on a new set of tires, there's likely a market maven in your community who can help.

In the social media era, we have Information Mavens whose social and professional networks are sources for connections that yield economic benefits to those who are fortunate enough to connect through their Information Maven. So, make a note that Lance Allred is achieving greater status as a thought leader while at the same time he's becoming a savvy and sought-after Information Maven.

At the End of the Day it's about SALES

Whether you're selling a product, an idea, or yourself, every part of the ACCESS Model is part of a sales formula. Authors want to sell more books, speakers want to get more speaking engagements, ministers want more people in their congregations, lawyers want more high profile clients ... the list goes on.

If you've cultivated a relationship with your target audience from the beginning and made them stakeholders, you'll be in a better position to ask them for their business. If you've really done a good job of creating stakeholders, you'll find these people recommending you and your product and even sharing news and information that originates from you.

If you do the math, you can quickly see how 500 trusted connections (on any social media platform) who recognize your thought leadership and have a stakeholder relationship with you or your brand, can reach 150 who can reach 35 who can reach 5. Before you know it, you could have 2.7 million people who either recognize you as a thought leader or are on a road to doing so.

It's not easy, but it's probably not as hard as a deaf kid from a polygamous commune in Montana making it to the NBA and playing with LeBron James.

About the Author: David K Brake is the CEO of The Grandview Group, a company that helps organizations ideate, validate, and create compelling content and products for their target markets. He is the coauthor of the business best-seller, **The Social Media Bible 1/e** (Wiley, 2009), where the ACCESS Model was first introduced.

"A Space Shuttle Tile, A Philosopher, A New Life Form & My Good Friend, Lance Allred"
Dave Murray

Why do we remember certain things so vividly, but forget others? For the folks that study these things, most think it depends on the emotional impact of an event. A first kiss, an injury, a special vacation, saying "I do", the birth of a child or even the death of a loved one, are all vivid memories that many of us share.

But what about the ones we don't have in common; the ones unique to ourselves or just a few others? It wasn't until I met Lance Allred and watched his TEDx talk, *"What is Your Polygamy,"* that I discovered the striking reason why a handful of my memories are inextricably linked.

A little over thirty-five years ago, on April 12, 1981 (I had to look it up, my memory isn't *that* good) My ten-year-old self sat riveted, along with millions of others around the world, watching the Space Shuttle Columbia rocket its way into orbit. Almost twenty years in the making, it was hailed as one of humankind's greatest achievements. I was excited. It was amazing. Even at ten, I recognized its monumental significance.

Interestingly, the launch isn't the Space Shuttle memory that holds the most sway in my brain. About a year before Columbia launched, my classmates at J.E. Cosgriff Memorial in Salt Lake City, Utah were treated to a very special show-and-tell by a classmate's dad. Mr. "Shuttle Dad" led one of the teams responsible for developing the tiles that made it possible for the shuttle to return to Earth. This was a big deal. Stories about these tiles had been all over the news.

So, imagine my surprise when Mr. Shuttle Dad pulled out an actual tile! I was overwhelmed and in awe.

165

But what happened next was a complete surprise, he brandished a blow torch and asked the teacher to turn off the lights. He ignited the torch, went to work on the bottom of the tile and explained the science behind what we were witnessing. In seconds, the tile glowed a reddish-orange and illuminated our classroom. One by one he asked us to come up and put our hands on the opposite side. The bottom radiated with heat, but it was still cold on the other side. The experience was something uniquely special. I was inspired. I wanted to learn more. I still do today.

About ten years later, while plodding my way through some of my prerequisites at the University of Utah, I found myself sitting in Professor Fred Hagen's World Religions' class. A friend of mine had told me to absolutely take a class from Professor Hagen if I had the opportunity. Little did I know how my friend's suggestion would impact my life.

Until this time, I'd never experienced a teacher like Professor Hagen. He was astoundingly brilliant, subtly irreverent, extraordinarily inspiring and never used notes. One of my all-time favorite Professor Hagen stories is something he recounted during a very stormy morning on campus. According to Professor Hagen, it happened a few years before during a lecture about Nietzsche. A thunderstorm was raging over campus and menacing claps of thunder were nearly synchronous with his comments about some of Nietzsche's anti-Christian views. At one point, a bolt of lightning struck so close, the whole classroom instantaneously shook. Not one ever to neglect the natural pageantry of what had just unfolded, Professor Hagen picked up his umbrella, nonchalantly walked to the window, started jabbing towards the sky and yelling, "you senile old son-of-a-bitch, you missed me again, your aim must be getting worse!" Unsurprisingly, a few students were offended by his remarks and brought them to the attention of the department head. The department head took it to the Dean of Humanities and the dean summoned Professor Hagen to his office.

166

Professor Hagen told us he listened intently as the dean lectured him about responsibility, reminded him about the amount of money students were spending and scolded him about unnecessarily insulting their beliefs. Silent to this point, Professor Hagen interjected and asked the dean a question, "And what beliefs are those, Dean?" "Well, you know," the Dean says, "most students at this University are Christians and we can't have you blaspheming during class." Calmly, he responded to the dean's point, "Surely, Dean, the merciful God of Christianity wouldn't throw lightning bolts. It's Zeus who throws lightning bolts and I was addressing him." The dean abruptly ended the meeting and thanked Professor Hagen for his time.

I took as many classes from Professor Hagen as I could -- whether I needed them or not. His lectures and stories were legendary and still shape my life today. I knew then, as surely as I know now, anyone who had the good fortune of experiencing a Fred Hagen lecture was experiencing something fantastically rare. I was inspired. I wanted to learn more. I still do today.

In 2007, I watched my first TEDx Talk, *My Creations, A New Form of Life,* by Theo Jansen. In an instant I was mesmerized. I showed it to any friend who might be interested -- and even some who weren't. I made my family watch it. I shared it as much as I could. The story was riveting and the video -- exquisite. In it, Jansen demonstrates his especially life-like kinetic sculptures built from old plastic tubes and lemonade bottles. These sculptures (or "Strandbeests" as he calls them) roam Holland's coastlines "feeding on wind and fleeing the water." And according to TED, "each generation of his Strandbeests is subject to the forces of evolution, with successful forms moving forward into new designs." Immediately, I wondered how I'd never heard about TED before this moment. No matter, I was hooked. TEDx Talks became a staple at my house. Their branding, "ideas worth sharing," was perfectly accurate. Watching talks from some of the world's leading minds, innovators, personalities and artists was invigorating, powerful and reminiscent of feelings I'd had before. I was inspired. I wanted to learn more. I still do today.

I met Lance Allred for the first time in the fall of 2016. Lance needed some public relations and marketing help and a mutual friend had suggested we meet. Straightaway, we hit it off. He was passionate, sincere, honest, confident, insightful, kind and had an extraordinarily unique story. He teared up telling me about his life. I was moved and without hesitation knew this was someone I HAD to help. The world needed to hear him. We needed his insights. I told him I would do what I could to help publicize his about-to-be-released TEDx talk and I sent him this text later that night, "Just wanted to say thanks again. I didn't have any expectations today, but I was genuinely moved by you and your story. You're a very impressive individual and I look forward to helping you find ways to connect your message to the world."

A few weeks later, he sent me an email with a link to the talk after it was published. Again, I sent him a text, "Just sitting on a bench and waiting for my son to get in some last fly casts before heading home... As it turns out, it couldn't have been a more perfect place to watch your video. It's powerful, evocative, funny, sincere, compelling and amazing!... Very glad to have you in my life. Look forward to helping you."

What I've never fully shared with Lance (until now) was how profoundly his talk impacted me. For the first time in my life I finally understood why memories of the space shuttle, my philosophy teacher, and a TEDx Talk by Theo Jansen were linked. Lance's talk challenged me to consider why I believe and think the things I do, and in that moment, on that bench, watching my son fly fish at sunset, I asked myself a question I'd never asked: Is there a reason I feel emotional connection between memories? As it turns out, there's a simple reason and I have Lance to thank.

What I felt at ten years old, what I felt in college and what I felt ten years ago was all the same. Being around people who push discovery, challenge convention, tackle new ideas and move the world forward is exhilarating and emotional. I've been fortunate enough to have first-hand experience with some these people. Lance is the latest.

How does all of this relate to delivering a TEDx Talk that's viewed a million times or more? TED and TEDx talks are fundamentally about people like those above; people who inspire, push discovery, challenge convention, tackle new ideas and move the world forward. TED's greatest value is giving the world on-demand access to some of the best of among us... a lesson I learned from Theo Jansen. So where do you fit? How will you frame your talk? How are you unique? Be real. Be raw. Be relevant. Don't give the audience what you think they want, give them you. Give them your unique self. They'll be inspired. They'll want to learn more. They won't forget you.

- Dave Murray
Marketing Guru/Consultant
President of Atlys TV

"Heal Thyself"
Dr. Jaynee Poulson, PhD

When I first met Mr. Allred, we literally bumped into each other. True story. We were at a charity event sitting at adjacent tables next to equally important, albeit rival, companies. When the awards were over, everyone stood up to mix, mingle, eat, and network. Now instead of handing me a card like several other executives did that day, Lance did something powerful and memorable. He grabbed my pen and wrote his name, cell phone number, and email into my journal. This becomes an important point that I will refer back to later because it's how I believe I heal myself. Fast forward to today: I am President of L Squared Productions LLC, with Lance Allred CEO, providing inspirational content and motivational public speaking and publishing, along with college curriculum development, and consulting and leadership training to corporations, schools and nonprofits. --Years ago I worked as a licensed mental health counselor, licensed professional counselor and K through 12 educational counselor.

When I watched "What is your Polygamy?" I loved it, because it was rare to have the complex made simple, to have an authentic voice address complex issues and have uncomfortable conversations brought up. I didn't hear just the word polygamy–I think that word could be replaced with any word. You fill in the blank. It's a universal message.

Polygamy brings forward that universal message, which is even more ironic right? What is your polygamy? Are you willing to ask yourself that question? I think you could fill in the blank with a safer word, what is your baggage? What is your story? What is your perceived truth? What is your ego based decision, that keeps you in the thought patterns that form your current reality? What is your comfort zone consisted of?

The question is universal and one that I fear we don't ask ourselves enough. What are the things that hold us back from Loving ourselves? Taking risk? Pursuing our dreams? Feeling safe? Knowing our worth?

So now this is my part of the book and it is my pleasure to ask you to go on the journey you started with the adult Lance Allred to achieve your own Million view Tedx talk. To do that you must dig deeper, which perhaps really begins back with the little five year old Lance, figuring out two of the most difficult things we all must learn throughout our journey to SELF LOVE, ACCEPTANCE, and ACTUALIZATION (the highest state of Maslow hierarchy of needs). Allowing your true self to be heard, so you can then become the greatest communicator in the world.

So let's begin. Here is the way to truth: what is your _____?

As a means of finding your voice, your true self, and your "polygamy" you will need a journal. Like the one Lance wrote his information in that I carried that day. I personally had mine with me in my hands and carry one everywhere. At this point, it feels like a survival tool. I have them from when I was a little girl, boxes of them. I write my way out of rooms and calm myself down while in some of them. I write regularly in my journal. It's cathartic. A true outlet of free expression and (until my brilliant editor gets a hold of my articles, blogs, etc) it is like this "Dr. Jaynee of old, releasing these streaming thoughts of mind-blowing uncensored crazy town," population: ME.

It's almost as though I am being paid back for all those years I assigned thousands of girls to write in their "therapy journals." Go ahead and roll your eyes but I called it their "Home Fun" instead of homework. Yep, I really did! I am such a believer in all things positive that I refused to be associated with any additional adult delegated paperwork to be done during home hours, so it was "fun" that I assigned–and yes, to me it had a very big distinction. My therapeutic office was the world in which I created, so let me break it down for you... in their language (minus the hashtags), if they thought it was lame, or even worse yet, "work," to be completed at home thereby making it "homework," I might as well not even ask. And more importantly, if what I assigned them was "fun" then I've overcome half the battle, right?

Look, I know they pseudo hated it, but I also knew it helped heal them while they explored their developing identities, found their own voices and got on their path of recovery. I was willing to call it whatever cheesy thing necessary to get their thoughts onto those pages. Journaling works. It helps, it heals. It's a fact. So they needed to do it. I am suggesting you start there.

Ok, so keep reading, and more to my point.... Start WRITING! For an example, the streaming thoughts are running wild in my head and heart, jumping from place to place, begging to be constructed, foundation pouring out in Jane Austen style of sharp wit, well, pour–your soul out until there is nothing left and you think you are enchanted like Emily Dickinson, because that's when you become more lovely than you hoped or imagined; from the telling of your story, you become powerful beyond measure. When you journal you need not edit yourself or spell check; flow, free write, express yourself. It's part of the process. Groove, beat-box, rhyme like a rapper at the mic, flow like a river. Rock out to the beat of you, freestyle!

There is such strength in writing and courage in telling, and I have found that when I remain silent, I am lost. Whenever I think back and recall the girls that sit nervously in my office sharing with me a glimpse into their world, I am still in awe of the pure unwavering hope and belief in that first moment; that if they told me what they thought in the deepest parts of themselves, if they gave their dark hidden secrets away, that maybe, just maybe, I might know how to help them. They would trust and tell me their pain... can you even imagine how strong they had to be in that moment? Because had they been silent, stayed silent, if they never trusted anyone: all hope would be lost. They were bold girls. Powerful young women. Fearless. They trusted enough to let a stranger, me, into their world. How blessed I was. How grateful I am for their courage. We can take inspiration from that and write down our words. The ones that could not trust, those that didn't share, that never wrote, those were the few I was never able to reach; no one was able to help them while they remained in silence unwilling to help themselves.

In fact, women talk of this throughout history and literature. When their voices have been silenced, they have been driven to the point of madness. My point is this: when you tell me to be silent and still, I will move and shout! That registers in my brain as a threat to my spirit, which is unacceptable to me. I am not in the bell jar. I know why a caged bird sings, and I have never killed a mockingbird.

That being said, I never once, in all those years asked any girl to do anything I wasn't willing to do myself. I journaled. So here is an outline for you to journal and ask your "self" what your polygamy is so you can find your *authentic* voice.

Let Lance's words help you unpack the baggage you might be carrying that makes it difficult to speak your own truth. Read these questions and write down your answers in your journal, no need to edit, don't worry about grammar and punctuation. This isn't a test, this is just to get it out of your head and connect with your heart.

Find a quiet place and take a few deep breaths.

--You are on this journey to find: what is your_____blank_____? (polygamy)

Let's start by looking at what's familiar to you, "the devil you know." What is the devil you know?

What have you always been told or believed that has structured your thought patterns and beliefs?

What's the world you grew up in like?
What keeps you safe?
What keeps you safe from pain?
What's your familiar hell?
What's an unfamiliar heaven?

What are the thought patterns you accept and live by, that you inherited in your childhood?

Think of those perceived truths as creating a comfort zone. What are the boundaries that exist? Do they keep you safe? Free? Protect you or Cage you?

Are you acting out of Fear? Or acting out of Love?
They're only two fears we are born with: the fear of falling and the fear of loud noises. Others are ego-based fears. What are the fears that you've created? That keep you from taking risk?

What are the Utopian dreams that you believe in?

What is the black and white thinking in your life? The all-or-nothing expectations?

Is there something you would do anything to protect? If so, how does that limit or hinder your growth? Or help your success?

Do you have absolute truth? Absolute certainty? Do you need to be right? Are you feeling safe?
Do you play mental gymnastics, creating two opposing truths that contradict each other in your life? And if so, What are the paradigms that need to shift?

Do you have to earn love? Is love unconditional?

Are you so special? Do you have to do everything right? Can we ever be perfect?

Can you choose clarity?   What's a mental prison for you?

Can we truly be Empowered? I have... I need... I should....

What does empowerment mean to you?

Turn this into voice of empowerment using voice of choice and accountability....
I will.... I choose..... I choose to be a leader of my own life!

If we are actors on our own stage, called the Stage of Life and we are not acted upon, are you being accountable?

Are you a leader of your own life?

Are you being accountable?
Are you acting with integrity?
Do you show Compassion?
Can you sit with discomfort and failure?
Are you truly the leader of your own life?

Choices are based on thought patterns and past behaviors. By writing things down you have a chance to take a look at your most honest self and dialogue with a rough form of "you" privately to perhaps see something you might not have considered before. Finding your "polygamy" will be an opening to your faults and can be used as a tool to motivate you to take action, discover new challenges, while learning new reasons to help believe in yourself and see you as you truly are without the conditions of societal pressures, work stress, family expectations, so you can face up to the outside challenge as your best self. Then you will be in the space to stand and deliver the TEDx Talk you envisioned as your truest self.

There are literally hundreds of doctors, philosophers, I could quote from proving why it will help you find your polygamy and give a better TEDx Talk to journal. You can google it but I'll save you some time and summarize here and offer three points.

1. Oprah writes in a journal every day. Enough said. :-)

2. Scientific evidence supports that the act of writing accesses your left brain, which is analytical and rational. Then while your left brain is busy, your right brain is free to create, intuit and feel. In sum, writing removes mental blocks and allows you to use all of your brainpower to better understand yourself, others and the world around you. Maud Purcell, LCSW, CEAP

3. I go back to what Spencer W Kimball said in 1975 in the New Era: *"Get a notebook, a journal that will last through all time and maybe the Angels may quote from it for eternity. Begin today and write in it. Yor going and coming, your deepest thoughts, your achievements and your failures."*

I quote him because he says to write down your *failures* and he references that Angels may quote from them for eternity. I like the thought of Angels quoting and referencing our failures! Sometimes we forget how important our failures are and that they are of equal importantance as achievements and to our comings and goings and our deepest thoughts and matter as much to the creating of the person we become. He said your achievements and your failures. Achievements are equal to our failures and the Angels would quote from them just the same. That is so powerful to me. Not to forget our failures, or deny them, lie about them, or run from them but learn from them and allow them to be written down for the angels to quote from because they didn't leave those out, they're necessary to the learning process, they're needed to teach us, to humble us, to help us grow and if we don't write them down with honesty and share them with authenticity, then we will not reap the full benefit of the great rewards from journaling.

Dr. James W. Pennebaker, a professor in the Department of Psychology at The University of Texas at Austin and author of several books including Writing to Heal: A Guided Journal for Recovering from Trauma and Emotional Upheaval, has spent 20 years encouraging people to spend 15 to 20 minutes a day for a few consecutive days writing down their deepest feelings. Pennebaker helped pioneer a study of individuals using expressive writing as a method of healing. He found that short-term focused writing can benefit all types of people, from those dealing with a terminal illness to victims of violent crime to first-year college students.

In Writing to Heal, Pennebaker says, "People who engage in expressive writing report feeling happier and less negative than before writing. Similarly, reports of depressive symptoms, rumination, and general anxiety tend to drop in the weeks and months after writing about emotional upheavals."

About Health listed a few scientifically proven health benefits:

Journaling decreases asthma, arthritis, and other stress related health conditions; Increase cognitive functioning, it strengthens the immune system, it counteracts stress, it helps to notice your feelings, it connects you to your heart. And I would like to add, it helps you find your Polygamy, speak your truth and give an authentic TEDx Talk.

My sample Journal -

"I've been writing for hours this week when this Mom has been driving back and forth to California for more Cancer treatment for my Mom. Then my world stood still after I took my oldest for what should have been a quick physical to play high school basketball. Instead I was told after an abnormal ECG that he had an arrhythmia, right bundle branch block,

possible murmur, and needed to see a cardiologist. So I took my sophomore son, that had newly been voted the team co-captain, to interrupt his varsity practice and tell his coach he would not be playing basketball until further notice. Suddenly, I felt like I was in the middle of a cheesy after-school special. I stood there trying to remember my lines for the role of the mother.

Although I was alone, shocked, and confused all I knew for certain in that moment was that I would do whatever my child needed, but that I had absolutely no idea what that was going to be and there was nothing that could be done until Monday. So over the weekend, he went to the Birthday party of a friends while I worked on appointments.

I had not thought about the party again until Wednesday while I was sitting in yet another doctor's office this time watching my son have an ultrasound of his heart, and he gave me his phone because his younger brother was playing games on it. I started flipping through the phone, and read messages accusing me of having breathalyzed him when he came home, calling another mother and "ratting" out the other boys for drinking. They were calling him a nark, a snitch, and so forth.

After confronting my son he pleaded with me to remain silent about it and even as the words came out of his mouth they were like water to my green skin. I felt myself melting as images of my daughter's future diplomas instead of our mothers' bras were burning before my eyes, (and yes, of course, I know they never actually burned their bras, come on, I teach Intro to feminism but the imagery is what comes to mind).

He literally was begging me to not talk to anyone or say anything, even though when he showed up to school on Monday and sat down at lunch, his friends got up and left the table all at the same time like some 80's movie. Cue music, and try to image him there at the table scrabbling to explain as they walk away... turning their backs to him.

Wait, I did what?... she called who? ....huh? And on the Monday after he's told he has heart problems? After he can no longer play the game he loves? Oh, if only Cindy Mancini could have walked in and dumped him like she did Ronald in *Can't Buy Me Love* with that slap across the face, the movie montage from the 80's would be complete.

However, wouldn't it stand to reason that it was not the time to be messin' with my child? And surely I shouldn't be forced to wear a Scarlet Tattletale letter on my Chest that I did in no way earn? Because again, could this doctor please heal herself already! ... so my old life can stop returning back into my new one, Ironically enough, I did that once in my professional career. I stood at the "meeting of the crossroads" between feminism and legality. Where I was once accused of something I did not do and instead of fighting or defending myself at all in any sort of way, I was silent and still. I gave up on myself and all that I believed in and worked for and just thought if you think I'm guilty until proven innocent and it's an uphill climb forget it. I'm not spending my children's college fund on the battle. So I surrendered, I gave up. I figured it wasn't worth the fight and my dignity was better served in not fighting. It was after I had retired and was staying home. I gave up my license, years after I had sold my practice. Because I was too arrogant to go defend myself and stand and be judged which only made me appear more guilty.

At the time it didn't seem relevant because I had already retired and it didn't matter to me what people said or thought but it should have and it does on principle now. I would stand up for myself and admit what I did do wrong and then say, "hold up, no, I didn't do that, or this, and I for sure didn't ever do that, but I did do those things and I am sorry for this" or just say something! Speak... defend. I would not repeat what I assumed at the time was just the easier better way because not making a decision was making a decision.

So at the end of my son's appointment, I learned that he does not have a bad heart and I am grateful.

And I will not be bullied into being silent about anything ever again. Call me whatever name you like, just don't call out my son for something he didn't do because that is a lesson I learned can have long term lasting effects. He needed friends at that table and not the kind Julius Caesar had.

As fate would have it, he played in the basketball game that Friday, and there is video footage of an interview where I told him that night that he had been cleared to shoot the "lights out" our code, and to play with all his heart that night, and he did. Against his rival team in our small town, he hit a half court shot with three seconds left in the game to win and those same so called friends rushed the court, then carried him on their shoulders while chanting his name. It was the perfect end to the worst after school special I was ever a part of in my life.

When I started writing that journal above, did you see the beginning from the end? Did you know where I was going? And how it all would end? If you did please reach out to me and fix my life and you don't need this book or any book.

See, I thought while writing I would travel to my future, that I was writing about my day. My son. His heart. The doctor. His friends. It was about that, true, but it seems as though I keep intersecting with my past, can you see that?

Well, THAT is the beauty of journaling. Patterns will begin to emerge. So write it all down, you can't just say, "oh, no. I have coffee with my girlfriends and I talk to them and tell them everything," you need to see it written down. Never underestimate the clarity granted to you while you sort out things in your head during the process of writing it (even the visual style of your writing has meaning; it all matters). While writing about that coffee with your girlfriends you will become clear on why that conversation helps you, heals you and gives you the clarity you need to face your day.

Perhaps you'll see a theme develop. Mine might be the "Doctor Heal Thyself" path, a road of learning by teaching, growing, giving, serving, helping others. I suppose mistakes will be made; that's bound to happen as you travel along this particular type of road, Oh, you know the road? It's where you find your truth, even if you stand alone. And on this road you can scream, shout, dance, cry, laugh, but you will never, no, no, never you can not silence your voice, because I believe if you take the road, this journey- period- it will make all the difference in finding your powerful true voice and authentic tone for your TEDx Talk.

See, case in point, I've proven my own hypothesis. I made a difference in my life just now by writing this with the hopes of healing my own troubled soul over two issues I shared. One, a time when I was silent and surrendered relating that to how I felt when my son asked me to again give up my voice. Journaling allowed me to deal with it outside myself on paper and work through it as I dealt with my personal feelings over my past and my son's heart.

Now, please, speak your truth, groove to your own beat, listen to the deep feelings inside, and write it all in your journal. Allow Lance's words to help you find your own. Find your Polygamy, as a step in the process of speaking your own truth. Use your voice to become a powerful leader in your own life!

• Dr. Jaynee Poulson, PhD
Gender and Women's Studies
President of L Squared Prod.

PART 3
Coaching and Editing TEDx Talks

TEDx Submission-
Michael Page

Lance -

Here is an initial draft. It's too long - it's over 400 words and needs to be less than 300, but I'll reduce it. I just wanted to get your initial take on the proposal...

-

Hearing loss is a birth risk factor, which for years exceeded the prevalence of other maladies we've screened for for decades! In 1982, Utah became a leader in the identification of hearing loss in new born infants since the implementation of new born hearing screening for all infants, partially through the efforts of Karl White, Michael Cevette, and others.

Cochlear Implantation has been approved by the US FDA since 1985. Since then, in this brave new world, there has been a literal and emotional firestorm about the ethics and morality of implanting infants with deafness. There is nearly a religious fervor about a child's right to choose, and a parent's lack of responsibility in severing a deaf child from its natural deaf culture by implantation. Some even suggest taking deaf children from their hearing parents and allowing the children to be raised by deaf parents.

Spoken language experts suggest that there is a critical window of time where implantation is necessary in order to capitalize a child's right to listening and spoken language. They claim that every child with deafness will require the earliest intervention in order to maximize their opportunities for education, employment, and independence. Decisions about cochlear implants in infants, they claim must be made long before a child is old enough to choose. Otherwise it's too late.

What's ethical? What's moral? And what's the impact of either choice. Should society play a role in the decision since state and federal funds are used to support infants on either side of the decision?

Credible data continue to come forward about the impact or lack of cochlear implants in infants, as well as "societal costs of deafness" by those who remain in their deafness. The data are compelling:

Credible research suggests:
1. 90% of deaf children are born to hearing parents.
2. Because listening and spoken language skills are time sensitive, the optimal time for implantation is at or prior to one year of age, or within months of identification of deafness. By the time for a child to decide, it's too late.
3. 98% of all cochlear implant users would "do it again," even with associated challenges.
4. Device failure rates are less than 1% after ___ years.
5. The median (not average) reading level of deaf (unaided/unimplanted) high school students is at the 4th grade level.
6. Most hearing parents of deaf children never learn sign language to a conversational level.
7. Children with cochlear implants
8. Lifetime Societal costs of children with deafness who are identified in infancy are estimated to be over $1M per child.

In this brave new world of social freedom and equality, the interplay of ethics and morality penetrate not the decisions of infants, but those of parents, health care providers and language experts. What would you do?

Lance edit -

Michael, Try this. 297 words.
-

In 1985, Utah was the first state to implement mandatory hearing screening for infants. In this same decade, Cochlear implants were approved by the US DA.

Since then it has been a zealous debate regarding the ethics and morality of implanting infants with deafness, comparable to the fervor we see in defense of religious freedom.

The blowback and judgment is so pitted regarding the parents' individual choice if they wish their deaf child to assimilate into the hearing world, even to the point of suggest taking deaf children from their hearing parents.

There is a critical window where implantation is necessary in order to capitalize a child's right to listening and spoken language, maximizing their opportunities for education, employment, and independence. Decisions about cochlear implants must be made before a child is old enough to choose.

What's ethical? What's moral? And what's the impact of either choice? Should society play a role? Should parents be able to so flippantly remove options from their child? Is that ethical? Shouldn't the child be entitled to decide when they are old enough?

1.   90% of deaf children are born to hearing parents.
2.   98% of all cochlear implant users would "do it again".
3.   The median reading level of deaf (unaided/unimplanted) high school students is at the 4th grade level.
4.   Most hearing parents of deaf children never learn sign

language to a conversational level.

5.   Lifetime Societal costs of children with deafness who are identified in infancy are estimated to be over $1M per child.

6. The socio-economic gap for the deaf community is well below the national average. **(I heard this at AG Bell. Is this true?)**

With social freedom and equality at the forefront of national discussion, should parents be able to so absolutely determine their child's path and quality of life?

What would you do?

"Shots"
A TEDx Draft
Bosten Van Der Veur

-This is a submission from Bosten, a college athlete, to Lance Allred, for feedback on TEDx Talk draft, to which Lance will edit and revise in latter half of chapter.

I believe life is all about opportunity and challenges. Life being a game of chance does not present equal opportunity or challenges for everyone. However, I do think that everyone gets an opportunity an is faced with some kind of challenge. Maybe 1, maybe 10, maybe 100. But I think everyone gets at least one of each. One opportunity to change everything. One challenge that can throw everything off track. One shot to really make a dream a reality. Or one nightmare that can turn your whole world upside down. I will often refer to these opportunities and challenges throughout our lives as "shots", being a basketball player it helps make it a lot simpler. I'm sure you can apply it to whatever interest in life you are pursuing. I wanna talk about different opportunities, challenges or shots that I have been given in my life. One of the first major "shots" in my life is actually a literal one. When I was a toddler I was diagnosed with Juvenile Rheumatoid Arthritis. Around 300,000 kids have some sort of arthritis or rheumatic disease. I struggled to walk as a youngster and often times my mother would have to escort me out to the play ground with her and help me use the different play ground equipment. She would carry me from the slide, to the jungle gym, to the monkey bars. Wherever I was trying to go she would help me get there. This is a perfect example of how people can create opportunity for you or help you get out of a rut. But I'll come back to that later. When I was six I received my first cortisone shot. I still remember it too this day. For whatever reason they didn't put me under any kind of anesthetic. The nurses and my mother had to pin me down while the doctor stuck what seemed like a 9 inch needle at the time directly into my right knee. I remember screaming in pain and tears running down my face. This "shot" was one of the major set backs in my life. I loved playing sports and being active, since a very young age. My knee problems made this very difficult for me. I even blew out my knee while trying to balance football, basketball, and baseball.

I can assure you my mom wouldn't even let me dream of playing three sports again after that. But I even wore a knee sleeve or brace for a good chunk of my high school career. This was a huge challenge for me, especially trying to be the athlete I wanted to be in high school. But I wouldn't allow it to stop me from seizing opportunity in my high school youth. My knee would swell and glow red after some practices and I would ice my knee and seek extra attention from the trainers after practice or school. Thankfully I was able to grow out of my JRA toward the end of my senior year. But some challenges can take a lot of time to overcome. It is important to stay positive during difficult times, like when the light at the end of the tunnel seems impossible to reach. I often told myself after a hard set during a workout that the pain wouldn't last forever and eventually I would be fine. I found this fairly translatable to many other areas in life. No pain last forever, time heals all things.

Sophomore year is where my second major "shot" of life took place. I had worked extremely hard during my freshman offseason and was determined to have a solid sophomore year. After an ok regular season, it was conference time and we were playing our rivals at our house to kick things off. A perfect opportunity to make a statement and start the conference off strong. After a grueling game in one of the most fun environments I have ever been a part of. We were down two with three seconds left on the clock. The ball was put into my hands and I threw up a half court prayer. Somehow it went in and for the next two years I was known as the kid who made "the shot". Not everyone gets an opportunity to make a game winner against there rival but if you do then you have to be willing to shoot it. To be ok with whatever the outcome. You can't be afraid to shoot the shot because you might miss. And I believe that there are many different "the shot" moments for everyone in life. A test you have to take to make or break a grade. A job application that could change your families life. Even something as simple as building up the courage to go talk to a girl. Who knows! Maybe she is your future wife. The point is that you have to be willing to seize those opportunities and not let the fear of a negative outcome stop you from taking the chance. You will hear people that have accomplished great things often talk about the immense number of times that they failed. That it didn't work out. That they took there shot and missed. But it didn't stop them from shooting again and again and again. Another thing I want to touch on briefly is not allowing yourself to get caught up on one small victory. Lets say I just stopped practicing after I made that buzzer beater. I was content with what I had accomplished and felt like I could just ride that wave as far as I wanted to go. What if all I sent coaches when they asked for film was the video of me making that one shot? Do you think anyone would have recruited me? No, often times we can be recognized by one great shot in our life but its the hundreds, even thousands of other shots we took before that that even made the one big shot possible. Don't allow yourself to get frustrated with defeat, but be wary of being blinded by victory.

After my high school career ended, I moved to Northern California to continue playing basketball. This time I was playing for Columbia College, a junior college in the small town of Sonora. This provided many new challenges and opportunities alike. But it was also where I stubbled upon another one of my "shots". We were college kids in a small town and jumped at the sign of being able to do anything fun. It was mid early October and a couple teammates and I got wind of a party not to far from our apartments. We decided to make the trip even though we had practice early the next morning. As we pulled into the house and walked through the front door we immediately noticed the uneven guy to girl ratio. With only about five girls at the party, there were at least 15 guys not including us four. What made things worse is they were mostly made up of firefighters from the fire academy at Columbia. The problem with this was that there was some kind of unspoken beef between the basketball players and the firefighters at Columbia. Something that had happened in past years and basically just established a "we don't like each other" kind of relationship. Regardless of being out numbered and in bad company, we were determined to have a good time. Being college students, there was alcohol involved and a small altercation ensued around midnight. The situation involving myself, my teammates, and a few of the firefighters was defused quickly and things continued on as normal. Around 2 o'clock that night as things began to die down, another incident began to take form. The mixture of alcohol and desire to show who was in charge eventually escalated into a shouting match between my roommate and a firefighter. I quickly tried to grab two of my teammates and motioned to our designated driver that it was time to go. He got the message and helped me try to escort everyone outside. Once outside we really noticed how outnumbered we were and that this was not a fight that was worth getting into. I watched as my roommate swung at a firefighter near him and stepped to grab him before everything went black. I woke up in the hospital with several stitches on the side of my left eye and a broken jaw. I was blindsided by a "shot" thrown from one of the firefighters. Sucker punched from behind in my very first fight. My jaw was wired shut and I was unable to eat solid food for around 6-7 weeks. I drank every kind of smoothie you can imagine. From peanut butter and jelly to pizza flavored. I lost 15 pounds and missed the first 3 games of my college career indefinitely. Once I was back in shape and caught up with my team I had missed nearly 6 games. It was extremely difficult to communicate with anyone and I began to sink into depression. I tried to stay as positive as I could and drank whatever I needed to so I wouldn't lose as much weight and could help my team as soon as possible. I spent extra time with my trainer doing jaw exercises in hopes of trying to make a quicker recovery. I would not have made it back to my normal self if it wasn't for the support of my teammates, my mother, and my coaches mother who took care of me and who I am very grateful for to this day. It was a huge setback for me that I would never wish on my worst enemy. Though this was an example of a challenge I overcame in my life. I want to touch briefly on how the challenges we face can affect others in our life as well. Even the people who seem to present the challenges. I decided to press charges on the person who hit me which lead to an investigation since no one actually saw who hit me.

I am certain that some of the people there witnessed who hit me but no one wanted to rat on there friend. Eventually the officers that were on my case gave up because they couldn't get anyone to say who had hit me, therefore there was no one to charge with the assault. I let it go and decided that it wasn't worth my time to continue trying to bring justice to my cause. I was actually informed of who exactly hit me almost a year later. I had since transferred to another school and it was one of the friends I had made at Columbia who lived and grew up in Sonora that text me one day and told me that she overheard people talking about that night and they said the name of the kid who hit me. Having already put it in the past, I thanked her for letting me know and continued on with my week. A couple weeks passed and I received another call, this time from a former teammate. We engaged in small talk for a short while before he dropped the bomb on me that he learned that the kid who had broke my jaw so long ago had died in a drunk driving accident. I was shook by the news and began to think about if I could have done more to prevent this. Maybe by not closing the case and eventually finding out who had done this I could have given him an opportunity to get off this destructive path. Maybe if his friends had come forward and told the cops what happened, he would have changed his ways and would still be alive today. The point I'm trying to make is that doing the hard thing, the thing that doesn't seem like the "cool" thing to do. May be the right thing to do for that person. Avoiding a challenge doesn't make it go away and can sometimes make things even worse further down the line. You have to be willing to face your challenges and accept the result because we can't see whats up ahead. You have to trust the process and be ok to fail and take a negative consequence sometimes. God has a plan for all of us and he doesn't give us more than we can handle. I believe that and I believe that its ok for everything not to go what you think is the "right" way. If you allow yourself to get caught up on one tree, you could miss seeing the rest of the forest. Have faith that if you fail, it will only make you stronger and remember it could also end up saving your life.

To conclude I just wanna say thank you to everyone in my life that has either given me an opportunity or helped me through a challenge. I am grateful for you and for God for allowing me to take advantage of opportunity and persevere through challenges. I would also like for everyone to keep in mind that there will always be someone out there that has it worse off than you do. Don't get caught up in your own challenges. Be aware that other people are struggling to, it's not just you. Look for the opportunity to help others in there challenges and lighten their load. If you ever feel overwhelmed then I find it helpful to stop thinking about yourself for just a second and go help someone else. You'll find that your problems aren't so big after all. I would also like to say that you must pounce on opportunities. Because you truly do not know how many you are going to get. Do not look at any opportunity like it is to small to care about or to large to handle. Do the little things and take on the big things. Opportunity is the thing that separates ordinary people from extraordinary people. You have to be willing to capitalize on opportunity and risk failing. But always fail forward, take something away from your failures and use it to progress. I hope that this talk got you thinking about different opportunities you can take advantage of and gave you hope for the challenges you will face. Thank you.

Lance Allred Edit of "Shots" -

~~I believe life is all about opportunity and challenges.~~
Like a basketball game, life is a game of chance and does not present equal opportunity or challenges for everyone. However, ~~I do think that~~ everyone gets an opportunity ~~an is faced with some kind of~~ in the midst of their challenges if they stick with it. Maybe 1, maybe 10, maybe 100. ~~But I think everyone gets at least one of each~~.

One opportunity to change everything.

One challenge that can throw everything off track.

One shot to ~~really~~ make a dream a reality.

Or one nightmare that can turn your whole world upside down.

I ~~will often refer to~~ call these opportunities and challenges throughout our lives as "shots." , Being a basketball player it helps make it a lot simpler.

~~I'm sure you can apply it to whatever interest in life you are pursuing. I wanna talk about different opportunities, challenges or shots that I have been given in my life.~~

One of the first major "shots" in my life is actually a literal one. ~~When I was~~ As a toddler I was diagnosed with Juvenile Rheumatoid Arthritis. Around 300,000 kids (Per year? Or in the US Total?) have some sort of arthritis or rheumatic disease.

I struggled to walk as a youngster and often times my mother would ~~have to~~ escort me out to the play ground with her and help me use the different play ground equipment. She would carry me from the slide, to the jungle gym, to the monkey bars. Wherever I was trying to go she would help me get there.

This is a perfect example of how people can create opportunity for you or help you get out of a rut. ~~But I'll come back to that later.~~

When I was six I received my first cortisone shot. I still remember it too this day. For whatever reason they didn't put me under any kind of anesthetic. The nurses and my mother had to pin me down while the doctor stuck what seemed like a 9 inch needle at the time directly into my right knee. I remember screaming in pain and tears running down my face. This "shot" was one of the major set backs in my life. I loved playing sports and being active, since a very young age. My knee problems made this very difficult for me. I even blew out my knee while trying to balance football, basketball, and baseball.- ~~I can assure you my mom wouldn't even let me dream of playing three sports again after that. But I even wore a knee sleeve or brace for a good chunk of my high school career.~~ This was a huge challenge for me, especially trying to be the athlete I wanted to be in high school. But I wouldn't allow it to ~~stop me from seizing opportunity in my high school youth.~~ stand in my way.

~~My knee would swell and glow red after some practices and I would ice my knee and seek extra attention from the trainers after practice or school.~~ Through years of swelling, pain and inflammation, thankfully I was able to grow out of my JRA toward the end of my senior year. ~~But some challenges can take a lot of time to overcome. It is important to stay positive during difficult times, like when the light at the end of the tunnel seems impossible to reach.~~ I was able to get through so much of that pain by telling myself after a hard set during a workout that the pain wouldn't last forever and eventually I would be fine. I found this fairly translatable to many other areas in life. No pain last forever, time heals all things.

Sophomore year is where I refer to my second major "shot". ~~I had worked extremely hard during my freshman offseason and was determined to have a solid sophomore year.~~ After an ok regular season, it was playoff time and we were playing our rivals which of course meant it was a grueling game in one of the most fun environments I have ever been a part of.

We were down two with three seconds left on the clock. The ball was put into my hands and I threw up a half court prayer. Somehow it went in and for the next two years I was known as the kid who made "the shot". Not everyone gets an opportunity to take or make a game winner against their rival but if you do then you have to be willing to shoot it. To be ok with whatever the outcome. You can't be afraid to shoot the shot because you might miss. You have to be willing to fail. If not, you are sending a message to the universe that you don't those shots. And I believe that there are many different "the shot" moments for everyone in life. A test you have to take to make or break a grade. A job application that could change your families life. Even something as simple as building up the courage to go talk to a girl. Who knows! Maybe she is your future wife. The point is that you have to be willing to seize those opportunities and not let the fear of a negative

outcome stop you from taking the chance. Again you have to be willing to fail. You will hear people that have accomplished great things often talk about the immense number of times that they failed. That it didn't work out. That they took their shot and missed. But it didn't stop them from shooting again and again and again.

Another thing I want to touch on briefly is not allowing yourself to get caught up on one small victory. Lets say I just stopped practicing after I made that buzzer beater. I was content with what I had accomplished and felt like I could just ride that wave as far as I wanted to go. What if all I sent coaches when they asked for film was the video of me making that one shot? Do you think anyone would have recruited me? No, often times we can be recognized by one great shot in our life but its the hundreds, even thousands of other shots we took before that that even made the one big shot possible. Don't allow yourself to get frustrated with defeat, but be wary of being blinded by victory. **(It is valid point, maybe even stating the obvious and not crucial to your message. Make every word count. You want to be under 13 minutes. I promise.)**

After my high school career ended, I moved to Northern California to continue playing basketball. This time I was playing for Columbia College, a junior college in the small town of Sonora. ~~This provided many new challenges and opportunities alike. But it was also where I stubbled upon another one of my "shots".~~ Here is where my "Third" life altering shot occurred. ~~We were college kids in a small town and jumped at the sign of being able to do anything fun.~~ It was mid early October and a couple teammates and I got wind of a party not to far from our apartments. ~~We decided to make the trip even though we had practice early the next morning. As we pulled into the house and walked through the front door we immediately noticed the uneven guy to girl ratio. With only about five girls at the party, there were at least 15 guys not including us four. What made things worse is they were mostly made up of firefighters from the fire academy at Columbia. The problem with this was that there was some kind of unspoken beef between the basketball players and the firefighters at Columbia. Something that had happened in past years and basically just established a "we don't like each other" kind of relationship. Regardless of being out numbered and in bad company, we were determined to have a good time.~~

(Details. Not always important. It is the idea that is important. TED: Ideas worth spreading.)

Being college students, there was alcohol involved. ~~and a small altercation ensued around midnight. The situation involving myself, my teammates, and a few of the firefighters was defused quickly and things continued on as normal.~~ Around 2 o'clock ~~that night as things began to die down, another incident began to take form.~~ the mixture of alcohol and desire to show who was ~~the alpha~~ eventually escalated into a shouting match between my roommate and a firefighter. I quickly tried to grab two of my teammates and motioned to our designated driver that it was time to go. He got the message and helped me try to escort everyone outside. Once outside we really noticed how outnumbered we were and that this was not a fight that was worth getting into. I watched as my roommate swung at a firefighter near him and stepped to grab him before everything went black

Unaware of the time that had passed, I woke up in the

hospital with several stitches on the side of my left eye and a broken jaw. I was blindsided by a "shot" thrown from one of the firefighters. Sucker punched from behind in my very first fight. My jaw was wired shut and I was unable to eat solid food for around 6-7 weeks. I drank every kind of smoothie you can imagine. From peanut butter and jelly to pizza flavored. I lost 15 pounds and missed the first 3 games of my college career ~~indefinitely~~. Once I was back in shape and caught up with my team I had missed nearly 6 games. It was extremely difficult to communicate with anyone and I began to sink into depression. ~~I tried to stay as positive as I could and drank whatever I needed to so I wouldn't lose as much weight and could help my team as soon as possible. I spent extra time with my trainer doing jaw exercises in hopes of trying to make a quicker recovery.~~ I would not have made it back to my normal self if it wasn't for the support of my teammates, my mother, and my coaches mother who took care of me ~~and who I am very grateful for to this day.~~ It was a huge setback for me that I would never wish on my worst enemy. ~~Though this was an example of a challenge I overcame in my life. I want to touch briefly on how the challenges we face can affect others in our life as well. Even the people who seem to present the challenges. I decided to press charges on the person who hit me which lead to an investigation since no one actually saw who hit me. I am certain that some of~~
~~the people there witnessed who hit me but no one wanted to rat on there friend. Eventually the officers that were on my case gave up because they couldn't get anyone to say who had hit me, therefore there was no one to charge with the assault.~~ Because no one was willing to testify against the man who took his "shot" against me, the local police would not file charges. I let it go ~~and decided that it wasn't worth my time to continue trying to bring justice to my cause. I was actually informed of who exactly hit me almost a year later. I had since transferred to another school and it was one of the friends I had made at Columbia who lived and grew up in Sonora that text me one day and told me that she overheard people talking about that night and they said the name of the kid who hit me.~~

~~Having already put it in the past, I thanked her for letting me know and continued on with my week. A couple weeks passed and I received another call, this time~~ A year later I received a call from a former teammate. ~~We engaged in small talk for a short while before he dropped the bomb on me that he learned that~~ who said that the kid who had broke my jaw ~~so long ago~~ had died in a drunk driving accident.

I was shook by the news and began to think about if I could have done more to prevent this. Maybe by not closing the case and eventually finding out who had done this I could have given him an opportunity to get off this destructive path.

Maybe if his friends had come forward and told the cops what happened, he would have changed his ways and would still be alive today. The point I'm trying to make is that doing the hard thing, the thing that doesn't seem like the "cool" thing to do, is a shot we either choose to take or not. Sadly many people choose not to shoot that shot, which is still a missed shot, because you miss every shot you don't take. ~~May be the right thing to do for that person. Avoiding a challenge doesn't make it go away and can sometimes make things even worse further down the line. You have to be willing to face your challenges and accept the result because we can't see whats up ahead. You have to trust the process and be ok to fail and take a negative consequence sometimes. God has a plan for all of us and he doesn't give us more than we can handle.~~ No bearing testimonies on TEDx Talks. ~~I believe that and I believe that its ok for everything not to go what you think is the "right" way. If you allow yourself to get caught up on one tree, you could miss seeing the rest of the forest. Have faith that if you fail, it will only make you stronger and remember it could also end up saving your life.~~ No time for all this, while all valid points, they are clichés. TEDx Talks, people want new ideas.

~~To conclude I just wanna say thank you to everyone in my life that has either given me an opportunity or helped me through a challenge. I am grateful for you and for God for allowing me to take advantage of opportunity and persevere through challenges. I would also like for everyone to keep in mind that there will always be someone out there that has it~~

worse off than you do. Don't get caught up in your own challenges. Be aware that other people are struggling to, it's not just you. Look for the opportunity to help others in there challenges and lighten their load. If you ever feel overwhelmed then I find it helpful to stop thinking about yourself for just a second and go help someone else. You'll find that your problems aren't so big after all. I would also like to say that you must p

Take your shots when they come your way because we never know how many we are going to get. Whether make or miss, it doesn't matter. The most important thing is to try, and pick yourself up and keeping playing on. Because you truly do not know how many you are going to get. Do not look at any opportunity like it is to small to care about or to large to handle. Do the little things and take on the big things. Opportunity is the thing that separates ordinary people from extraordinary people. You have to be willing to capitalize on opportunity and risk failing. But always fail forward, take something away from your failures and use it to progress. I hope that this talk got you thinking about different opportunities you can take advantage of and gave you hope for the challenges you will face.

Thank you.

-

Bosten, good job. We need an "action point." You have a great story and did a great job with the "Shot Theme." We now need an action point, that gives the listener some applicable tool or behavior or act that can help them shift into this mentality of never being afraid to fail, and to take the shot.

Think on it and be clever. It may seem mundane to you, but a lot of people aren't athletes and so something mundane to you may be really different for their mentality.

Remember, the idea is the most important thing. While telling people to never not take their shot, to always be willing to fail, is inspiring… it isn't a "new idea."

My TEDx Talk was a different strain from my professional keynotes of inspiring people. My TEDX talk I had to find something that everyone could relate to, their inherited thought patterns and comfort zones. And then I gave them the "action point" of "choose to be a leader of your own life" with learning to speak by saying, "I choose to go to school to day, " instead of "I have to go to school" etc...

You have something here. You just have to give a little extra, and dig down and turn your story from being just an inspiration story, to a teaching opportunity.

Think on it for a few days and get back to me. Write it all again, consider the edits and contractions. Less details, more idea worth spreading. There is something in here and we will find it.

Less is more.

You want the audience thinking about their experiences, your experiences are just a catalyst for them to go inward and take their own journey. Your job is to help the listener learn more about themselves, not learn about you.

Remember, people remember what they feel, not what they hear. We will find the action point. And also, the "idea worth sharing." Stay Tuned.

Lance

Critiquing an Existing TEDx Talk:
"We Will Go On Loving Ourselves"
Kambridge Van Der Veur

-Kambridge is a collegiate athlete who spoke at TEDxYouthParkCity in 2015.

A few years ago, as a junior in high school, I was given the opportunity to present a TEDxYouth Talk through Park City High School in Utah.

I had very little to work with and blindly just went with an idea, paying no attention to many things that I now know to think about or consider after having met Lance Allred and conversed with him.

Based off of "How to Give the Million View TEDx Talk," I definitely wish I had done a few things differently, or asked myself these questions in the process of preparing and preforming my talk.

What is your idea?

Originally, when I first heard of the opportunity to try out for a spot in the TEDxYouth Program with my high school I was stuck. I knew I wanted to do something different, and since preforming poetry is something I love to do, I wondered why I couldn't approach the talk from a more artistic stand point. Since the audience was entirely composed of high school students, teachers, and parents, I decided to specifically direct my message to them. I realize now that my talk missed the mark on a key point: sure, I may have brought a new perspective to the stage, but I didn't bring any new ideas. Self-love has been preached about for ages, and my purpose was to shed more light on how society encourages the opposite. Although I'm proud of the perspective I performed, I feel it lacked new ideas the audience could walk away inspired by.

Lance: Kambridge, I wouldn't say the audience wasn't inspired. I commend you for doing something different. It was the first "Poetry Slam" style TEDx Talk I had heard. A+ for originality.

Is there heart, soul, and head in your talk?

I know there is heart and there is soul, because I remember how I felt on the stage. It takes some of my head to remember and speak in poetry, no? So, I would say I have all three. Did the audience learn anything new? Maybe, but moreso, maybe I just got them to think. At least I hope so.

Lance: You had all three. However, we feel the passion, but did we get to know you? You speak of "we" in the poem, because you are speaking for others who do not have a voice, which takes great courage and leadership. But, do we really get to know Kambridge?

Have you researched your audience?

My audience turned out to be a main factor in how the message behind "We Will Go On Loving Ourselves" developed. As I mentioned earlier, I knew I would be speaking to students around my age, as well as the parents of the other speakers. I wanted the kids in the audience who had ever felt victim to harsh or mindless judgement from others to feel that they were not alone, and that they have something to stand for against this judgement. I wanted the parents in the audience to understand their role in this judgement as well.

Lance: I agree, that it was the right audience, with Utah Teen Suicides at a national high.

Have you researched your topic? Is it original?

I researched my topic, but not nearly enough, or on the correct platform. Yes, some information as well as the story included where researched, but I didn't search for other talks just like mine. What did I find when I did? There are hundreds of slams on self-acceptance and society's influence. Hundreds.

Mine is only a rendition of this concept of a whole, an addition to the masses. The biggest marker that separates my topic as spoken word from the others is that it is done as a TEDx Talk and not in a traditional slam setting. This goes back to finding a new idea that will have the audience having an Aha! moment, something that I seemingly lacked. But all things considered, I do not recall any TEDx talks being addressed in poetry slam form.

Lance: As stated above, A+ on originality.

Do you have mentor?
I did not have a mentor in preparation for my talk. (I wouldn't know how to even go about how to find a mentor/who and why they would fit?)

Lance: Being a "youth speaker" at the time and at the whim of adults and parents, this is a hard one. One could find an online speaking coach, or other life or executive coach, over the internet, and they would be able to give feedback. But don't overthink this one. I have had many, many people give me horrible advice, and thankfully, at the end of the day, I have always chosen to go with my gut... hindsight, growing pains and all.

Have you let other people review and revise your draft?
When I first tried out with my poem, it was very much a rough draft. Letting other people read my work, just on paper and without preforming it, helped me establish a final draft I was proud of.

Letting someone simply read the words you will say doesn't allow for distractions in how well you may present the information. I had three people (barely enough in my case, as I wish it had been more) read the rough and final drafts, and give me honest and constructive feedback. I can say this was a very, very important step in my experience because it helped me actualize my message from different perspectives and fresh platforms.

Lance: Did you perform in front of them? A draft is one thing, but I allowed many people to critique my performance delivery before the big day? I don't suggest ever getting this kind of feedback from family, as they will never be fairly objective, positive or negative.

*Have you recorded yourself giving the talk and critiqued yourself?

This is something I really wish I had known to do. It's like hearing yourself sing – it rarely sounds the way you thought it would. Every time I re-watch my TEDx Talk I can make a list of what I wish I had done differently. If I had gone into the preparation of my talk knowing to record myself to review it, I may have caught these mistakes before I made them permanently.

Lance: This is one of the things I am most grateful that I thought to do. Truly. It allows you to be in the seat of the observer. The film/tape never lies. Ever. And now you know this, for all of your future public speaking endeavors!

*Is your title memorable and searchable?

Sadly, the title of my TEDx Talk was one I didn't get a say in. There was a miscommunication between who uploaded my talk and myself concerning the title I had originally given it. It was originally titled "Ode to Those", which I personally think fits as a title to the poem but not specifically a TEDx Talk. This is where I realized research can come into play! If I could name it again, I would watch other TEDx Talks and see where their title was derived.

Lance: Yes, this is frustrating. Thankfully, my rhetorical question, "What is your Polygamy?" was the cog on which the whole presentation spun, and was provocative, their was no question from me or the committee what the title was going to be. But I also have other fellow speakers, who submitted their title request, but the committee went ahead and gave them different names. Title is everything, and I am sorry for anyone who doesn't have a voice in their own title.

*Have you found the perfect wardrobe?
Is there a platform to judge this? I can tell the thought process I put into this but don't know if my wardrobe is good/bad??

Lance: Stay gold, Pony Boy.

*Do you have a set and practiced stage exit?
I wish someone had told me how to do this. I didn't even give it a thought at any point when preparing for my talk! It obviously shows in how abruptly I leave the stage after I finish speaking. I realize now that my final words would have held more effect if I had allowed the audience to take them in before rushing off stage.

Lance: You got off that stage faster than a cat out of bath, and I laughed, because it was endearing. And yet, I wished you could have allowed yourself to enjoy the moment just a little more. You deserved it. This has nothing to do with the viewership, it is simply me wanting the speaker to allow themselves a moment of pride and accomplishment. And you earned that.

*What are your pre-marketing and post-marketing plans?
This was another aspect that I completely overlooked. Why would I need to market? College?

Lance: Kambridge, marketing is everything! A successful TEDx talk, goes well on resume, school and job submissions, etc... Don't just use the TEDx talk like a bucket list that so many others do... fight for it. It is your dream, your voice. Like a relationship, a goal, a dream, you give it every chance you can to be heard by as many people who need to hear it. There are people who need to hear that talk. Help them find it! Marketing...

    P.S. You're my hero, Kambridge.

-Lance

PART 4

What is YOUR Polygamy?

"Mining the Walls"
Matt Langston

I found Lance Allred's TEDx Talk on YouTube on accident the fall of 2016; many views before the 2,702,486 it has at the time of me writing this. I couldn't say exactly when, I don't remember. I also have no idea how many times I have listened to this since, I would dare say it has been dozens of times at least.

I had never listened to a TEDx Talk before this one on purpose, and before I could realize what was playing en que, the questions were already there and I was pushed outside my little comfort bubble into a totally new playing field of why did I live in my comfortable hell, what lay outside it, and dare I leave it.

No one has ever before and nor have they since posed such a universal question to my existence as to why I accepted it as such and where was it headed. Needless to say, I listened to the entire message.

I have since then scoured the TEDx offerings in search of something that could top this, something to give me a more in depth question, something that could motivate me more and I found nothing close. I will get back to that a little later in this, but for now I would like to explore the meaning, the relevance to my life, and the depth of the cut this took to my soul.

I have enough official polygamy's to fill volumes, yet, in consideration of your sanity I will only refer to the largest of them, the one that tries to keep me in bed in the morning and awake at night. Insomnia sure, everyone has insomnia when they let it consume their minds; I see it as only a symptom of a disease, just another note on a chart scribbled down by someone without much thought as to why sleep finds not my mind. I could give every symptom of my polygamy and it

208

wouldn't match anyone else's that gained from this masterpiece because I might daresay no two people have watched this TEDx talk and received the same message.

My message was loud and clear, it is to this day and I fight it still. I am one of seven plus billion people spinning around in circles on this planet and if I want to find myself it will take looking right here, right inside myself.

No one wants to analyze themselves, it hurts like hell to tear down our walls and peek outside. There is no comfort in a personal prison system, and every human has perfected one of two things- Living inside our own self built prisons or exploiting the rest of humanity while imprisoned.

I don't know much about those that exploit others, I am not one of them and never will be. Neither is Lance as he offered a challenge to me personally to peek outside my walls, to become uncomfortable enough with myself to find myself and I have been ever since.

I search for a word to define my personal condition, my personal polygamy if I may, and only can say it is possibly that I care too much for those I shouldn't and not enough for the people that have made my life worth living.

Some days it may not seem much like anything in particular, I work with mostly inanimate objects, rock and dirt, sometimes precious metals, sometimes precious nothing. Twenty years ago I worked with people and very good people. After a couple of divorces and a few other happenings in life I found myself living in the middle of nowhere shopping at a convenience store late at night to avoid as much human contact as humanly possible. I had cancelled all outside sources of anything save the internet brought to my phone. I have finally faced my prison and be it brick by brick, one social interaction at a time, I am mining the walls and they are falling.

This is the beauty of the message and the message is universal to every single person on the face of this planet as we are all humans and we all have the same social disorders wired into our heads.

It is a survival instinct perverted by social conditioning that we will seek out those that satisfy what we want to hear, want to feel, and think what we already know to exist. This is exactly what I had done, except to the extremes of pushing everyone completely out, and locking myself completely in.

Needless to say, I'm not going to be a social butterfly anytime soon yet I have started rebuilding bridges long destroyed with my three children and their mother. I am employed in a job working with a crew of people and while I may still be playing in dirt, I now work with really good people which brings me back to why the message is so universal, and how I think it is different than any other one I have seen and why.

There are many TEDx Talks, many motivational speakers out there, and they want to motivate for a reason- be it fame or fortune. I could be wrong as I'm not too damn motivational most of the time and I don't look for motivational speakers either.

Lance Allred isn't a motivational speaker, meaning he pushes the listener into a place that isn't motivational at the moment nor is it comfortable. It puts your entire belief system whatever it may, right into your face, and it is absolutely terrifying for just a brief second until the fact is recognized that this can be conquered and the reward is great.

I don't know what the demographic breakdown of the listening audience is for the nearly 3 million times this video has been viewed but I would guess it consists largely of people that live by no extraordinary means, work with their hands and backs and minds, for in these people that I now have started to know and appreciate there is a longing for something that cannot be found in a belief system, a motivational rant, or a movie.

They are used to being pushed and used to pushing back. Every single day of every single week they work through physical and mental conditions that tear at the mind and every single day they come out winning in their professions. Their personal lives are left to the advice of waitresses and roughneck rants and they seek something they have no idea exists.

What is your polygamy? What is their polygamy? What stopped the world and asked that question? Thank you Lance Allred for being the one who asked this question. I'm sure you could have quadrupled your views being motivational and making the world warm and fuzzy, the measure of what you did instead, cannot actually be measured by anyone.

• Matt Langston
Vagabond,
Seeker,
Human Being

"My Miracle"
Kelli Davis

I love my friend Lance Allred but I'm kind of mad at him too!

I was getting along just fine living in denial and not dealing with my shit but after I listened to his Tedx Talk "What is Your Polygamy" I was forced to ask myself some big questions I didn't want to look at:

What belief systems am I trapped in?

What rules am I killing myself to live so God will be pleased with me?

What stories am I holding on to that paralyze me from moving forward?

Why do I choose to live in the prison created by belief system?

What thought patterns developed from my childhood are no longer serving me?

I have to admit, I didn't immediately ask myself these questions. I remember thinking it was a great talk, and that it could help me if I wanted to look at things, but I really didn't want to find out the answers to these questions. Instead, I at first just wanted to pick Lance's brain to see how I could give an amazing TEDx Talk, because I am an aspiring speaker. I just wanted to talk business. Again, I was doing just fine living in denial that I had much more work to do, in cleaning out my own closets before I could actually move into a space to help others.

I had figured out how not to feel my feelings for 20 years and I was really good at it! From the outside looking in I had the perfect life but on the inside I was dying because I wasn't willing to ask myself these questions.

Depression, anxiety, addictions and body dysmorphic disorder were symptoms of a much bigger problem. I was living in a belief system that no longer served me. I really thought I could continue to get away living like this but the universe intervened and opened me up in the most uncomfortable way possible… physical pain!

It happened on a very fateful day in December. I was driving home from Christmas break to see my family from Afton, Wyoming to Salt Lake City. I was in a very relaxed state listening to a podcast on my headphones when *BOOM!!!!*

I heard the loudest sound I had ever heard. I thought a bomb went off. I really had no idea at first if I was ok. It took me a second to get my bearings and realize that my sun roof had exploded in my car and I had glass everywhere. Thankfully, most of the glass went outside my car but I had it behind my back, in my passenger seat, on the floor and in the back seat.

I was so shocked that instead of pulling over I continued to drive 45 minutes home back to Salt Lake City. I didn't know it at the time but it was the universe's way of getting my attention. What could wake you up more than a physical explosion?

I really can't explain why but after my sunroof exploded chronic pain engulfed by entire body. After going to 20 different specialist and still not finding a solution to the pain I realized my body was offering me a gift, a solution to the emotional suffering that had plagued me for two decades. I was finally forced to look, really look at my religious beliefs that confined me in a box I never really fit in. I had to ask myself the scary questions.

Who am I? Does God really love me no matter what, especially if I don't live up to strict Mormon standards? Is it really true that God will punish me if I sin?

These and many more questions I had to address because I was killing myself to be perfect to please God and my parents.

Getting vulnerable and looking within can be very scary but it will save you as well!

Once I finally looked at these questions, I was able to strip away my beliefs to a very basic level and build a foundation that I knew to be true. I'm still figuring this out and it's a bumpy ride but I now chose to do things that feel true to me, not because I should do them or because I'm supposed to them, but because I actually believe in them. Freedom truly awaits on the other side of fear. When you push through the fears and ask yourself the tough questions, you can walk out of the prison you created, knowing you had the keys to open the door all along.

I host a podcast for Children's Miracle Network, Untold Miracles, where I get to explore the miracles of amazing children who fight vicious disease and illness everyday. They are truly miracles. And do you know what is also a miracle?

That I finally found the courage to ask myself the tough questions that no longer allowed me to live in denial.

That is a miracle. That is my miracle.

> • Kelli Davis
> Host: *Untold Miracles*
> Speaker
> Children's Miracle Network

"Wings"
NiKohl M. Cotton

I grew up in a single-parent household the only child of a black woman and an absentee father. My mother was often away from home because she had to work two, sometimes three jobs.

I had a multitude of babysitters that ranged from family friends to relatives but nothing was ever consistent. A consequence to having an absentee father meant that I had a few stepfathers most were good. But there is one that had the greatest negative impact on me.

My mother met a man in 1987, who was very abusive. He would often beat me for anything ranging from leaving dishes in the sink to making poor grades, which was anything less than an "A".

I was deathly afraid of him and my mother was, as well.

He was emotionally and verbally abusive to her, that he would constantly belittle her, while belittling me, too. I rarely saw my mother cry, but when her husband would have one of his "episodes," I would see her cry more often than I would like to. Things would get so bad that I would have to stay with different relatives.

Through all of this turmoil, my mother and I were forced to go to church, because my stepfather was a "spiritual" man, and like him, we pretended to be holy on Sundays.

Under the guise of religion, he would use Scripture to justify punishing me, to manipulate me in order to make me feel guilty about some of the things that I would do. If I had forgotten to wash a dish or didn't clean up my room, he would often quote scripture in order to make me feel guilty, or make me feel as though I had let God down and that I would be condemned to hell.

As a child, that is such a scary thought.

Even though my mother suffered through extreme emotional and mental abuse, she found the strength to tell the church leaders of all the abuse that she and I were suffering. Sadly, no one within the church would help use escape our own hell. Instead, they would offer us prayers and nothing else beyond that. I had never felt so trapped in my life! We were stuck in our own personal hell with no way out.

My mother and I endured this abusive relationship for approximately six years before she finally found the courage to leave. Having an abusive childhood caused me to experience a series of emotional roller coasters, which resulted in having trust issues especially in men or father figures.

I was always afraid that the next man in my mother's life would treat us the exact same way as my mom's previous husband. This was my polygamy.

Prior to starting high school, I was hardly encouraged to go to college but instead told to finish high school and find a good job. That's the potential people saw in me.

Finally, during my freshman year in high school, my mother met a man that who would eventually become my true stepfather, my "dad." Dad completely changed my perspective about going to college and told me that it was possible for me to attend. At that time, I didn't have any role models who ever attended college, so I had no idea what I was supposed to do to get started! I was breaking the chain. Before that, all I was ever told to aspire to, was get my high school diploma and get a simple job. After all, I was a poor black kid from a small town in Illinois who grew up in a single-parent household. I was the exact definition of a walking statistic. How dare I dream of anything different?

My academic advisor wasn't very forthcoming on how to apply for college, scholarships, or financial aid. But, he did manage to tell me how to get into the military.

I took the ASVAB or the aptitude entrance example in order to get into the military. I was admitted.

I was given "wings," and I left my small town and then I honorably served in the Air Force for 11 years.

After I got out of the military, I used my G.I. Bill to earn a bachelor's degree and I am currently in my Masters in Nursing.

The end of my polygamy came when I joined the military and I was able to escape my small town in Illinois.

The military enable me to travel and see the world! I was able to experience different cultures, meet different people, and get a new perspective on life. By being exposed to new things, I was able to escape the mentality that I was never going to be anything more than just a high school graduate working at whatever job I could find.

I ended my polygamy and I'm hoping that I've shown my daughter that accomplishing your goal is possible, no matter what. I am still working hard to ensure that my old chains remain broken. Through my life experiences, I encountered a lot of roadblocks that could have discouraged me from attending college or joining the military.

Although the information was not given to me, I have the knowledge for my daughter when she's ready to go to college. I haven't saved up money to pay 100% of her tuition, but I at least know what avenues to take so she can attend college. The last thing I want her to do is to become another statistic.

I don't regret anything that has happened in my life. I believe that it has made me the person I am today. It is because of this, I won't just settle for anything.

I will continue to push myself, spreading my wings, until I reach all of my goals. In life there will be obstacles in your path but what you will have to decide is whether r or not you will chose to get over those obstacles, or let the obstacles derail you from your path.

I do believe that you can do anything, if you set your mind to it. You just have to find your encouragement from within. Not from others, though it helps. I am so glad that I have broken my polygamy and that I am able to show my daughter a different way of life.

-NiKohl Cotton

What is <u>YOUR</u> Polygamy?

I asked Matt Langston, a fan who reached out to me online after watching my talk, to do me the honors of writing the very first submission into the "What is Your Polygamy?" franchise.

We are currently in the middle of talks and planning with David Brake and publishers to spin off "What is Your Polygamy?" into a podcast and book series, much like the Chicken Soup franchise.

With that, we are opening calls for your stories, your message, your triumphs and emotional battles and demons you have faced. We don't want your professional success story, but rather, your emotional and psychological success story. We want the world to know how brave you truly are.

Please submit your story at www.whatisyourpolygamy.com

You will get to call yourself a published author, if not a best-selling author.

Thank you for allowing the message to be heard and for sharing it with your loved ones.

Thank you for choosing clarity. And thank you for choosing to always move in gratitude.

-Lance Allred

About the Author

Lance Allred lives in Salt Lake City, Utah as a father to his son, Simon.

He travels the world as a keynote inspirational speaker, empowering corporations, nonprofits and schools on Leadership, Perseverance and Grit.

Watch his TEDx smash-hit, "What is Your Polygamy?" which has garnered over 3 Million Views in its first six months.

To learn more about Lance, and his TEDx coaching retreats visit his website, www.lanceallred41.com

L Squared Productions, 2017

Made in the USA
San Bernardino, CA
07 August 2018